MW00572334

Divorce
in Tennessee

*The Legal Process,
Your Rights, and What to Expect*

Eric J. Burch, Esq.

Addicus Books
Omaha, Nebraska

An Addicus Nonfiction Book

ISBN 978-1-938803-87-1
Typography Jack Kusler

This book is not intended to serve as a substitute for an attorney. Nor is it the author's intent to give legal advice contrary to that of an attorney. The information contained in this book is for general informational purposes only and should not be relied upon or considered legal advice applicable to a specific legal matter.

Library of Congress Cataloging-in-Publication Data

Burch, Eric J., author.
  Divorce in Tennessee : the legal process, your rights, and what to expect / Eric J. Burch, Esq.
    pages cm
  Includes bibliographical references and index.
  ISBN 978-1-938803-87-1 (alk. paper)
  1. Divorce—Law and legislation—Tennessee. 2. Alimony—Tennessee. 3. Custody of children—Tennessee. I. Title.
  KFT100.B87 2014
  346.76801'66—dc23
                                                    2014008200

Addicus Books, Inc.
P.O. Box 45327
Omaha, Nebraska 68145
www.AddicusBooks.com

Printed in the United States of America
10 9 8 7 6 5 4 3 2 1

Contents

Acknowledgments

I would like to thank all our clients who have entrusted me to guide them through the difficult process of divorce. By sharing your thoughts, questions, and concerns, you have given me an education over the course of the past fifteen years that is priceless. Without you, this book would not have been possible.

I acknowledge my partner, Trenena Stanley. Your contributions to our office and assisting our clients are nothing short of remarkable.

I extend my thanks to my legal secretary, Lisa Short. Your quick wit and kind demeanor immediately makes our clients feel at ease even though they are confronting some of the most difficult times in their lives.

I thank my office manager, Terri Trail. Eleven years ago, Terri and I started our office in one room with a computer and two card tables. Terri, I truly appreciate your dedication to this enterprise. I could not have done it without you.

I express my deep appreciation to my parents, Jack and Barbara Burch. You showed me the value of hard work and education from an early age. I could not ask for any better examples to follow.

Finally, I thank my wife, Melissa, and my children, Auggie, Abigail, and Sam who give me more joy than I could have imagined. Without your sacrifices of enduring long hours of my absence from home, my practice and this book would not be possible. I love you.

Introduction

I never tell anyone (with the exception of an abused spouse) to get a divorce. Divorce should be a last resort, particularly when children are involved. Divorce is one of the most difficult, agonizing things a person can experience. If a marriage can be saved, I recommend making every attempt to do so.

But, sometimes a divorce is the best course for a family. If a marriage is irretrievably broken, then staying together can be a worse alternative than breaking apart. Life is too short to be miserable. Chances are, if one spouse is miserable, the other spouse and the children are also miserable or soon will be.

The purpose of this book is to educate you about the divorce process in Tennessee. Most people who come to my office are paralyzed with fear of the unknown. I have found that giving clients as much information as possible about the process of divorce as possible eases their minds and helps them think through their options. Clients who are informed are able to make educated decisions about their future—nothing is more important than making good decisions about the future of your family.

This book is not intended to replace the advice of a good attorney. If you have retained an attorney to represent you in a divorce, that attorney will know more about the specifics of your case and the best way to help you through your divorce.

A divorce can seem like the end of the world. However, there will be finality eventually. The sun will shine and the flowers will bloom. You will get through it and come out the other side.

1

Understanding the Divorce Process

At a time when your life can feel like it's in utter chaos, sometimes the smallest bit of predictability can bring a sense of comfort. The outcome of many aspects of your divorce may be unknown, increasing your fear and anxiety. But there is one part of your divorce that does have some measure of predictability, and that is the divorce process itself.

Most divorces proceed in a step-by-step manner. Despite the uniqueness of your divorce, you can generally count on one phase of your divorce following the next. Sometimes just realizing you are completing stages and moving forward with your divorce can reassure you that it won't go on forever.

Develop a basic understanding of the divorce process. This will lower your anxiety when your attorney starts talking about "depositions" or "going to trial," and you feel your heart start pounding in fear. It can reduce your frustration about the length of the process because you understand why each step is needed. It will support you to begin preparing for what comes next.

Most importantly, understanding the divorce process will make your experience of the entire divorce easier. Who wouldn't prefer that?

1.1   What is my first step?

Find a law firm that handles divorces as a regular part of its law practice. The best recommendations come from people who have knowledge of a lawyer's experience and reputation. Even if you are not ready to file for divorce, call to schedule an appointment right away to obtain information about protecting

1

yourself and your children. Even if you are not planning to file for divorce, your spouse might be.

Ask what documents you should take to your initial consultation. Make a list of your questions to bring to your first meeting. Start making plans for how you will pay your attorney to begin work on your case.

1.2 Must I have an attorney to get a divorce in Tennessee?

You are not required to have an attorney to obtain a divorce in Tennessee. However, if your case involves children, alimony, significant property, or debts, you should avoid proceeding on your own.

A person who proceeds in a legal matter without a lawyer is referred to as *pro se,* on one's own. If you are considering proceeding without an attorney, at a minimum have an initial consultation with an attorney to discuss your rights and duties under the law. You may have certain rights or obligations you are unaware of. Meeting with a lawyer can help you decide whether to proceed on your own.

The Divorce Process

- Obtain a referral for a lawyer.
- Schedule an appointment with an attorney.
- Prepare questions and gather needed documents for the initial consultation.
- Meet for the initial consultation with attorney.
- Pay retainer to attorney and sign retainer agreement.
- Provide requested information and documents to your attorney.
- Take other actions as advised by attorney, such as opening or closing financial accounts.
- Attorney prepares complaint for divorce and affidavits for temporary matters for your review and signature.
- Attorney files complaint with clerk of the court. Attorney obtains *ex parte* orders if appropriate. Attorney obtains hearing date for temporary matters.
- Mandatory sixty-day or ninety-day waiting period begins when complaint is filed.

The Divorce Process (Continued)

OR

- Spouse is served papers by sheriff or process server.

- Negotiations begin regarding terms of temporary order on matters such as custody, support, and temporary possession of the family home. Attorneys prepare financial affidavits and child-support guidelines for temporary hearing.

- Temporary hearing is held.

OR

- Parties reach agreement on temporary order.

- Temporary order is prepared by one attorney, approved as to form by other attorney, and submitted to the judge for signature.

- If there are minor children, parties must attend a parent education class, develop a parenting plan, or participate in mediation.

- Both sides conduct discovery to obtain information regarding all relevant facts.

- Obtain valuations of all assets, including expert opinions if needed.

- Confer with attorney, identify issues, assess strengths and weaknesses of case, review strategy, and develop proposal for settlement.

- Spouses, guided by their attorneys, attempt to reach agreement through written proposals, mediation, settlement conferences, or other negotiation.

- Parties reach agreement on all issues.

- Attorney prepares decree and court orders for the division of retirement plans for approval by spouses and attorneys.

OR

- Parties prepare for trial on unresolved issues.

OR

- Trial preparations proceed and include the preparation of witnesses, trial exhibits, legal research on con-

The Divorce Process (Continued)

tested issues, pretrial motions, trial brief, preparation of direct and cross-examination of witnesses, preparation of opening statement, subpoena of witnesses, and closing argument and suggestions to the court.

- Meet with attorney for final trial preparation.
- Trial is held.
- Judge makes decision.
- Attorney prepares decree.
- Spouse's attorney approves decree as to form.
- Decree submitted to judge for signature.
- Judge signs decree of dissolution.
- Make payments and sign documents (deeds or titles) according to decree.
- Documents required to divide retirement accounts and ensure the payment of child support are submitted to the court.

1.3   Is Tennessee a *no-fault* state or do I need grounds for a divorce?

Tennessee, like most states, does not require fault for a divorce to be granted. If the parties are able to reach a settlement, the parties must only prove that irreconcilable differences exist between the parties. This is generally done by stating to the judge at the divorce approval hearing that efforts at reconciliation were made, that those efforts were not successful, that further attempts would not be beneficial, and that irreconcilable differences exist between the parties.

Although not required, if either party chooses to have a final hearing, then the testimony of either you or your spouse is likely to be sufficient evidence for the court to rule that the marriage should be dissolved. This testimony will state, as above, that efforts at reconciliation were made, that those efforts were not successful, that further attempts would not be beneficial, and that irreconcilable differences exist between the parties.

The judge may ask for information regarding the nature of the problems that led to the divorce or the type of reconciliation efforts made, such as counseling with a therapist or clergy member.

In cases where a settlement is not reached, the parties may stipulate that grounds for a divorce exist. If no such stipulation is made at the time of trial, the parties will submit proof of fault of one or both parties and the judge will grant the divorce to one of the parties against the other. Alternatively, the judge may just declare the parties to be divorced.

1.4 How will the judge view my or my spouse's infidelity?

In Tennessee, adultery is one of the grounds for divorce. In cases where property division or debt division is the main issue, the infidelity of you or your spouse is largely irrelevant. In cases of child custody, most judges frown on a parent who exposes a child to an extramarital affair. In cases where alimony is an issue, proving adultery, either through direct or circumstantial evidence, may be important. If it is proven, a judge will be more likely to award alimony if the other factors that support an alimony award are also present.

1.5 Do I have to get divorced in the same state I married in?

No. Regardless of where you were married, you may seek a divorce in Tennessee if the jurisdictional requirements of residency are met. The jurisdictional requirements are discussed in the following question.

1.6 How long must I have lived in Tennessee to get a divorce in the state?

Either you or your spouse must have been a resident of Tennessee for at least six months to meet the residency requirement for a divorce in Tennessee.

1.7 Can I divorce my spouse in Tennessee if he or she lives in another state?

Provided you have met the residency requirements for living in Tennessee for six months, you can file for divorce here even if your spouse lives in another state.

Discuss with your attorney the facts that will need to be proven and the steps necessary to give your spouse proper notice to ensure that the court will have jurisdiction over your spouse. Your attorney can counsel you on whether it is possible to proceed with the divorce.

1.8 My spouse has told me that she will never "give" me a divorce. Can I get one in Tennessee anyway?

Yes. Tennessee does not require that your spouse agree to a divorce. If your spouse threatens to not "give" you a divorce, know that in Tennessee this is likely to be an idle threat without any basis in the law.

There is case law in Tennessee to suggest that a judge should not leave two people married where one spouse no longer wishes to be married. While grounds for divorce must technically be proven if one spouse resists the divorce, a Tennessee judge will grant a divorce in almost every instance if one spouse comes to court seeking a divorce.

1.9 Can I get a divorce even when I don't know where my spouse is currently living?

Tennessee law allows you to proceed with a divorce even if you do not know the current address of your spouse. First, take action to attempt to locate your spouse. Contact family members, friends, former coworkers, or anyone else who might know your spouse's whereabouts. Utilize resources on the Internet that are designed to help locate people.

Let your attorney know of the efforts you have made to attempt to find your spouse. Inform your lawyer of your spouse's last known address, as well as any work address or other address where this person may be found. Once your attorney attempts to give notice to your spouse without success, it is possible to ask the court to proceed with the divorce by giving notice through publication in a newspaper.

1.10 I just moved to a different county within the state of Tennessee. Do I have to file in the county where my spouse lives?

The location where a divorce is filed is referred to as *venue*. In Tennessee, the proper venue is the last county where you and your spouse lived together. If one spouse moved into Tennessee from another state, then venue would lie in the county in Tennessee where the spouse moved.

1.11 I immigrated to Tennessee. Will my immigration status stop me from getting a divorce?

If you meet the residency requirements for divorce in Tennessee, you can get a divorce here notwithstanding your immigration status. Talk to your immigration lawyer about the likelihood of a divorce leading to immigration challenges.

1.12 Is there a waiting period for a divorce in Tennessee?

Yes. Tennessee has a mandatory sixty-day waiting period for divorces without children and has a mandatory ninety-day waiting period for divorces with children. This waiting period begins on the day the complaint for divorce is filed with the court.

1.13 What is a *divorce complaint*?

A *divorce complaint,* also referred to as a *complaint for dissolution of marriage* is a document signed by the person filing for divorce and filed with the clerk of the court to initiate the divorce process. Formerly referred to as a *petition,* the complaint will set forth in very general terms what the plaintiff is asking the court to order.

Sample Divorce Complaint

IN THE _____ COURT FOR THE _____
JUDICIAL DISTRICT AT _____, _____
COUNTY, TENNESSEE

JANE DOE,	)	
	)	
Plaintiff,	)	
	)	
vs.	)	No.
	)	
JOHN DOE,	)	
	)	
Defendant.	)	
	)	

Sample Divorce Complaint (Continued)

COMPLAINT FOR DIVORCE

PLAINTIFF WOULD RESPECTFULLY SHOW UNTO THE COURT THE FOLLOWING:
1.   Pursuant to the provisions of Tennessee Code Annotated, § 36-4-101, the Plaintiff submits the following statistical information:

HUSBAND'S NAME: (First, Middle, Last)_____

RESIDENCE-STATE_____COUNTY_____

CITY, TOWN OR LOCATION_____

STREET AND NUMBER_____

BIRTHPLACE (STATE OR FOREIGN COUNTRY)_____

DATE OF BIRTH (Month, Day, Year)_____

WIFE'S NAME (First, Middle Last)_____

MAIDEN NAME_____

RESIDENCE—STATE_____COUNTY_____

CITY, TOWN OR LOCATION_____

STREET AND NUMBER_____

BIRTHPLACE (STATE OR FOREIGN COUNTRY)_____

DATE OF BIRTH (Month, Day, Year)_____

PLACE OF THIS MARRIAGE-STATE_____

COUNTY_____

DATE OF THIS MARRIAGE (Month, Day, Year)_____

NUMBER OF CHILDREN EVER BORN ALIVE OF THIS MARRIAGE?_____

CHILDREN UNDER 18 YEARS_____

NUMBER OF CHILDREN UNDER 18 WHOSE PHYSICAL CUSTODY WAS AWARDED TO: ☐ No Children ☐ Husband ☐ Wife ☐ Joint (Husband/Wife) ☐ Other

PETITIONER ☐ Husband ☐ Wife ☐ Both

NAME OF PETITIONER'S ATTORNEY_____

ADDRESS:_____

RACE: HUSBAND_____WIFE_____

NUMBER OF THIS MARRIAGE: HUSBAND_____WIFE_____

IF PREVIOUSLY MARRIED, LAST MARRIAGE ENDED Specify)

HUSBAND:

☐ Not previously married ☐ by death ☐ by divorce or annulment

WIFE:

☐ Not previously married ☐ by death ☐ by divorce or annulment

EDUCATION - Specify highest grade completed

HUSBAND:

Sample Divorce Complaint (Continued)

☐ Elementary or Secondary ☐ College
WIFE:
☐ Elementary or Secondary ☐ College

2. Plaintiff and Defendant have resided in the State of Tennessee for more than six (6) months preceding the filing of this Complaint. The acts complained of were committed while the Plaintiff was a bona fide resident of the State of Tennessee.
3. Plaintiff alleges that the parties have experienced such irreconcilable differences in their marriage as would allow the marriage to be terminated under Tennessee Divorce Statutes.
4. In the alternative, Plaintiff alleges that the Defendant has been guilty of inappropriate marital conduct, such that cohabitation would be unsafe and improper.
5. In the alternative, Plaintiff alleges that the Defendant has been guilty of adultery.
6. The parties own certain real and personal property and have certain debts.
7. Plaintiff and defendant have_____children born of this marriage (Names, Date of Birth, Age)
8. The Plaintiff alleges that she is the fit and proper party to be named the primary residential parent of the parties' minor children, (names), and with reasonable visitation to Defendant and that Defendant is able bodied and capable of providing support.
9. The minor children have resided with the parties at _____ for the past ____ years. Complainant has not participated in any other litigation concerning the custody proceeding concerning the minor children herein in any court of this or any other state. Plaintiff does not know of any person not a party to this proceeding that has physical custody of the minor children herein or claims to have custody or visitation rights with respect to the minor children herein.
10. Plaintiff is unable to support herself financially and is in need of support, transitional, rehabilitative, pendente lite and permanently. Defendant, JOHN DOE, is able-bodied and capable of providing such support.

PREMISES CONSIDERED, PLAINTIFF PRAYS THAT:

1. That proper process issue and be served upon the Defendant, together with a copy of this Divorce Complaint, requiring him to appear and answer the allegations contained herein, but his oath

9

Sample Divorce Complaint (Continued)

to his answer is expressly waived.
2. That the parties be declared divorced from one another pursuant to T. C. A. §36-4-129(b).
3. That the Court approve a Marital Dissolution Agreement if entered into between the parties.
4. That at the final hearing the Court make an equitable distribution of the parties' debts.
5. That at the final hearing, the Court make an equitable distribution of the parties' real and personal property.
6. That at the final hearing, and in the event the parties are unable to enter into an agreement, Wife be named the residential parent of the minor children of the parties and this Court enter such orders as are appropriate relative to visitation, child support, health care, life insurance, etc.
7. That Defendant, JOHN DOE, be required to pay support, transitional, rehabilitative, pendente lite and permanently to Plaintiff.
8. For reasonable attorney fees and costs.
9. For such other, further, different and general relief to which she may be entitled.

JANE DOE

RESPECTFULLY SUBMITTED:

By: ERIC J. BURCH, BPR #019320
Attorney for Plaintiff
200 South Woodland Street
Manchester, TN 37355
(931) 570-2138
STATE OF TENNESSEE)
COUNTY OF COFFEE)

JANE DOE, after first being duly sworn according to law, makes oath that she has read the foregoing Complaint, that the statements made therein are true to the best of her knowledge, information and belief, and are made for the reasons stated and no other, and she believes she is entitled to the relief sought.

JANE DOE

Sample Divorce Complaint (Continued)

SWORN TO AND SUBSCRIBED to before me this the ____ day of _____, 20____

_____
NOTARY PUBLIC

My Commission Expires:_____

COST BOND

We go surety for costs of this cause under $500.00.

_____
ERIC J. BURCH

NOTICE TO BOTH PARTIES OF INJUNCTIONS IN DIVORCE

Pursuant to Tenn. Code Ann. § 36-4-106(d), the following temporary injunctions are in effect upon both parties upon the filing of a petition for divorce or legal separation, except on the sole grounds of irreconcilable difference, and upon personal service of the complaint and summons on the respondent or upon waiver and acceptance of service by the respondent with these provisions attached to the complaint and summons.

These temporary injunctions are in effect until the:

1. final decree of divorce or order of legal separation is entered,
2. petition is dismissed,
3. parties reach agreement, or
4. Court modifies or dissolves the injunction.

Both parties are restrained and enjoined from:

1. Transferring, assigning, borrowing against, concealing or in any way dissipating or disposing of, without the consent of the other party or an order of the court, any marital property; (Expenditures from current income to maintain the marital standard of living and the usual and ordinary costs of operating a business are not restricted by this injunction. Each party shall maintain records of all expenditures, copies of which shall be available to the other party upon request.)

Sample Divorce Complaint (Continued)

2. Voluntarily concealing, modifying, terminating, assigning or allowing to lapse for nonpayment of premiums, any insurance policy, including but not limited to life, health, disability, homeowners, renters and automobile, where such insurance policy provides coverage to either of the parties or that names either of the parties as beneficiaries, without the consent of the other party or an order of the court;

3. Harassing, threatening, assaulting or abusing the other and from making disparaging remarks about the other to or in the presence of any children of the parties or to either party's employer, and

4. Relocating any children of the parties outside the State of Tennessee, or more than 100 miles from the marital home, without the permission of the other party or an order of the Court, except in the case of a removal based upon a well-founded fear of physical abuse against either the fleeing parent or the child. In such case, upon request of the non-relocating parent, the Court will conduct an expedited hearing, by phone conference if appropriate, to determine the reasonableness of the relocation and to make such other orders as appropriate.

This does not in any way preclude either of the parties from seeking broader injunctive relief from the court.

1.14 My spouse said she filed for divorce last week, but my attorney says there's nothing on file at the courthouse. What does it mean to "file for divorce?"

When lawyers use the term "filing" they are ordinarily referring to filing a legal document at the courthouse, such as delivering a complaint for divorce to the clerk of the court. Sometimes a person who has hired a lawyer to begin a divorce action uses the phrase "I've filed for divorce," although no papers have yet been taken to the courthouse to start the legal process.

1.15 If we both want a divorce, does it matter to the judge who files?

In the eyes of the court, the *plaintiff* (the party who files the complaint initiating the divorce process) and the *defendant* (the other spouse) are not seen differently by virtue of which party filed. The court, as a neutral decision maker, will not give preference to either party. Both parties will be given adequate notice and each will have a chance to be heard and present argument. However, filing first can have certain procedural advantages. The spouse who files first is permitted to present their proof at trial first, submit discovery requests first, and file for temporary relief first. It is important to consult with your attorney regarding whether to file for a divorce first because each case is unique.

Discuss with your attorney whether there are any advantages to you filing first. Your attorney may advise you to file first or to wait until your spouse files, depending upon the overall strategy for your case and your circumstances. For example, if there is a concern that your spouse will begin to transfer assets upon learning about your plans for divorce, your attorney might advise you to seek a temporary restraining order to protect against such an action, without giving prior notice to your spouse. However, if you are separated from your spouse but have a beneficial temporary arrangement, your attorney may counsel you to wait for your spouse to file.

Allow your attorney to support you in making the decision about whether and when to initiate the legal process by filing a complaint for dissolution of marriage.

1.16 Is there a way to avoid embarrassing my spouse and not have the sheriff serve him with the divorce papers at his workplace?

Talk with your attorney about when, where, and how you want your spouse served. Often, your attorney can arrange to have a private process server, someone who is hired by the attorney, to serve the divorce papers at a specific time and location to minimize embarrassment. In some instances, sending the divorce papers by certified mail may be advantageous. In some relatively amicable situations, your spouse may come by your attorney's office and simply pick up the divorce documents.

1.17 Why should I contact an attorney right away if I have received divorce papers?

If your spouse has filed for divorce, it is important that you obtain legal advice as soon as possible. Even if you and your spouse are getting along, having independent legal counsel can help you make decisions now that could affect your divorce later.

After your spouse has filed for divorce, a temporary hearing can be scheduled at any time. It is possible you will receive only a few days' notice of a temporary hearing. You will be better prepared for a temporary hearing if you have already retained an attorney.

After you have received divorce papers, a written answer responding to your spouse's divorce complaint must be filed with the court within thirty days

1.18 What is an *ex parte court order*?

An *ex parte court order* is obtained by one spouse going to the judge to ask for something without giving prior notice or an opportunity to be heard by the other spouse.

With the exception of restraining orders, judges are reluctant to sign *ex parte* orders. Ordinarily the court will require the other side to have notice of any requests for court orders, and a hearing before the judge will be held.

An *affidavit*, which is a written statement sworn under oath, is usually required before a judge will sign an *ex parte* order. *Ex parte* orders are generally limited to emergency situations, such as requests for temporary restraining orders and protection orders.

When an *ex parte* order is granted, the party who did not request the order will have an opportunity to have an expedited hearing before the judge to determine whether the order should remain in effect.

1.19 What is a *motion*?

A *motion* is a request that the judge enter a court order of some type. For example, your attorney may file a written motion with the court asking for an order related to temporary custody, child support, parenting time, or financial matters, such as payment of bills.

Some motions are made to handle certain procedural aspects of your case, such as a motion for a continuance asking that a court date be changed or a motion for extension of time asking that the court extend a deadline. In some cases a motion may be made orally rather than in writing, for example when an issue arises during the course of a court hearing or trial.

1.20 Once my petition for divorce is filed, how soon can a temporary hearing be held to decide what happens with our child and our finances while the divorce is pending?

In most cases a temporary hearing can be held within thirty days of your divorce being filed with the court, assuming your spouse can be located to be given notice. The rules regarding temporary hearings vary between jurisdictions. For instance, some courts require mediation under local rules before a temporary hearing may be held. Consult with your attorney who is familiar with the local rules.

1.21 How much notice will I get if my spouse seeks a temporary order?

Tennessee law requires that you receive reasonable notice of any court hearings. In the case of motions for temporary orders, this notice may be as short as five days.

1.22 During my divorce, what am I responsible for doing?

Your attorney will explain what actions you should take to further the divorce process and to help you reach the best possible outcome.

You will be asked to:

- Keep in regular contact with your attorney.
- Update your attorney regarding any changes in your contact information, such as your address, phone number, and/or e-mail address.
- Provide your attorney with all requested documents.
- Provide requested information in a timely manner.
- Complete forms and questionnaires.
- Appear in court on time.

- Be direct about asking any questions you might have.
- Tell your attorney your thoughts on settlement or what you would like the judge to order in your case.
- Remain respectful toward your spouse throughout the process.
- Keep your children out of the litigation.
- Comply with any temporary court orders, such as restraining or support orders.
- Advise your attorney of any significant developments in your case.

By doing your part in the divorce process, you enable your attorney to partner with you for a better outcome while also lowering your attorney fees.

1.23   I'm worried that I won't remember to ask my attorney about all of the issues in my case. How can I be sure I don't miss anything?

Write down all of the topics you want to discuss with your attorney, including what your goals are for the outcome of the divorce. The sooner you clarify this, the easier it will be for your attorney to support you to get what you want. Realize that your attorney will think of some issues that you may not be thinking of. Your lawyer's experience will be helpful in making sure nothing important is forgotten.

Divorce Issues Checklist

Issue	Notes
Dissolution of marriage	
Custody of minor children	
Removal of children from jurisdiction	
Parenting plan	
Child support	
Deviation from child-support guidelines	
Abatement of child support	

Divorce Issues Checklist (Continued)

Issue	Notes
Travel expenses to facilitate parenting time for out-of-state parents	
Life insurance to fund unpaid child support	
Automatic withholding for support	
Child-support arrearage from temporary order	
Child-care expenses	
Child-care credit	
Health insurance on minor children	
Uninsured medical expenses for minor children	
Qualified medical support order	
Private school tuition for children	
College expenses for children	
College savings accounts for the benefit of children	
Health insurance on the parties	
Real property: marital residence	
Real property: rentals, cabins, commercial property	
Time-shares	
Retirement accounts	
Federal or military pensions	
Business interests	
Bank accounts	
Investments	
Stock options	
Stock purchase plans	
Life insurance policies	
Frequent-flyer miles	
Credit card points	

Divorce Issues Checklist (Continued)

Issue	Notes
Season tickets for events	
Premarital or nonmarital assets	
Premarital or nonmarital debts	
Pets	
Personal property division: including motor vehicles, recreational vehicles, campers, airplanes, collections, furniture, electronics, tools, household goods	
Exchange date for personal property	
Division of marital debt	
Property settlement	
Alimony	
Life insurance to fund unpaid maintenance	
Arrearage of alimony from temporary order	
Tax exemptions for minor children	
IRS Form 8332	
Filing status for tax returns for the last/current year	
Attorney fees	

1.24 My spouse has all of our financial information. How will I be able to prepare for negotiations and trial if I don't know the facts or have the documents?

Once your divorce has been filed with the court and temporary matters have been addressed, your attorney will proceed with a process known as *discovery*.

Through discovery, your attorney can ask your spouse to provide documents and information needed to prepare your case. Your attorney can also subpoena information directly from an institution to obtain the requested documentation.

1.25 My spouse and I both want our divorce to be amicable. How can we keep it that way?

You and your spouse are to be commended for your willingness to cooperate while focusing on moving through the divorce process. This will not only make your lives easier and save you money on attorney fees, but it is also more likely to result in an outcome you are both satisfied with.

Find a lawyer who understands your goal to reach settlement and encourage your spouse to do the same. Cooperate with the prompt exchange of necessary information. Then ask your attorney about the options of mediation and negotiation for reaching agreement. Even if you are not able to settle all of the issues in your divorce, these actions can increase the likelihood of agreement on many of the terms of your divorce decree.

1.26 Can I pick my judge?

Talk with your attorney about which judge may be the best fit for your case. While it is impossible to pick your judge in many instances, there is a choice in many jurisdictions regarding whether to file the divorce in circuit, chancery, or general sessions court. Your attorney should be knowledgeable regarding the tendencies of different potential judges. While it is difficult to predict exactly how a particular judge will rule on an issue important in your case, an attorney who has experience in litigating before each potential judge may be able to make a general prediction about how a judge would view your position.

1.27 How long will it take to get my divorce?

The more you and your spouse are in agreement, the faster your divorce will conclude. At a minimum, there will be a sixty-day or ninety-day wait from the date the complaint is filed.

Assuming all issues, such as custody, support, property, and debts, are completely settled between you and your spouse, if you so choose, a final hearing can be held after the waiting period. Otherwise, your decree can be submitted to the judge for his or her approval after the waiting period. However, your divorce will still not be "final" for all purposes.

1.28   What is the significance of my divorce being final?

The finality of your divorce decree, sometimes referred to as the *decree of dissolution of marriage,* is important for many reasons. It can affect your right to remarry, your eligibility for health insurance from your former spouse, and your filing status for income taxes.

1.29   When does my divorce become final?

Your divorce becomes final for different purposes on different dates. The date that triggers the time period for a divorce becoming final is the date that the divorce decree is entered by court. In most cases, this will be the day the judge signs your divorce decree.

For most purposes, your divorce is final thirty days from the date it is entered by the court.

1.30   Can I start using my former name right away and how do I get my name legally restored?

You may begin using your former name at any time, provided you are not doing so for any unlawful purpose, such as to avoid your creditors. Many agencies and institutions, however, will not alter their records without a court order changing your name.

If you want your former name restored, let your attorney know so that this provision can be included in your divorce decree. If you want to change your legal name after the divorce and have not provided for it in your decree, it will be necessary for you to undergo a separate legal action for a name change.

2

Coping with Stress during the Divorce Process

It may have been a few years ago. Or, it may have been many years ago. Perhaps it was only months. But, when you said, "I do," you meant it. Like most people getting married, you planned to be a happily married couple for life.

But things happen. Life brings change. People change. Whatever the circumstance, you now find yourself considering divorce. The emotions of divorce run from one extreme to another as you journey through the process. You may feel relief and be ready to move on with your life. On the other hand, you may feel emotions that are quite painful. Anger. Fear. Sorrow. A deep sense of loss or failure. It is important to find support for coping with all these strong emotions.

Because going through a divorce can be an emotional time, having a clear understanding of the divorce process and what to expect will help you make better decisions. When it comes to decision making, search inside yourself to clarify your intentions and goals for the future. Let these intentions be your guide.

2.1 My spouse left home weeks ago. I don't want a divorce because I feel our marriage can be saved. Should I still see an attorney?

It's a good idea to see an attorney. Whether you want a divorce or not, there may be important actions for you to take now to protect your assets, credit, home, children, and future right to support.

If your spouse files for divorce, a temporary hearing could be heard in just a matter of days. It is best to be prepared with the support of an attorney, even if you decide not to file for a divorce at this time.

2.2   The thought of going to an attorney's office to talk about divorce is more than I can bear. I canceled the first appointment I made because I just couldn't do it. What should I do?

Many people going through a divorce are dealing with lawyers for the first time and feel anxious about the experience. Ask a trusted friend or family member to go with you. He or she can support you by writing down your questions in advance, by taking notes for you during the meeting, and by helping you to remember what the lawyer said after the meeting is concluded. It is very likely that you will feel greatly relieved just to be better informed.

2.3   There is some information about my marriage that I think my attorney needs, but I'm too embarrassed to discuss it. Must I tell the attorney?

Your attorney has an ethical duty to maintain confidentiality. Past events in your marriage are matters that your lawyer is obligated to keep private. Attorneys who practice divorce law are accustomed to hearing a lot of intimate information about families. Although some information is deeply personal to you, it is unlikely that anything you tell your lawyer will be a shock.

It may feel uncomfortable for a short moment, but it is important that your attorney have complete information so that your interests can be fully protected. If speaking directly about these facts still seems too hard, consider putting them in a letter or e-mail from your private, secure computer.

2.4   I'm unsure about how to tell our children about the divorce, and I'm worried I'll say the wrong thing. What's the best way?

How you talk to your children about the divorce will depend upon their ages and development. Changes in your children's everyday lives, such as a change of residence or one parent leaving the home, are important to them and should be discussed. Information about legal proceedings and meetings with lawyers are best kept among adults.

Simpler answers are best for young children. Avoid giving them more information than they need. Use the adults in your life as a source of support to meet your own emotional needs.

After the initial discussion, keep the door open to further talks by creating opportunities for them to talk about the divorce. Use these times to acknowledge their feelings and offer support. Always assure them that the divorce is not their fault and that they are still loved by both you and your spouse, regardless of the divorce.

2.5   My youngest child seems very depressed about the divorce, the middle one is angry, and my teenager is skipping school. How can I cope?

A child's reaction to divorce can vary depending upon his or her age and other factors. Some may cry and beg for a reconciliation, and others may behave inappropriately. Reducing conflict with your spouse, being a consistent and nurturing parent, and making sure both parents remain involved are all actions that can support your children regardless of how they are reacting to the divorce.

Support groups for children whose parents are divorcing are available at many schools and religious communities. A school counselor can also provide support. If more help is needed, confer with a therapist experienced in working with children.

2.6   I am so frustrated by my spouse's "Disneyland parent" behavior. Is there anything I can do to stop this?

Feelings of guilt, competition, or remorse sometimes lead a parent to be tempted to spend parenting time in trips to the toy store and special activities. Other times, these feelings can result in an absence of discipline in an effort to become the favored parent or to make the time "special."

Shift your focus from the other parent's behavior to your own, and do your best to be an outstanding parent during this time. This includes keeping a routine for your child for family meals, bedtimes, chores, and homework. Encourage family activities, as well as individual time with each child, when it's possible.

During this time when a child's life is changing, providing a consistent and stable routine in your home can ease his or her anxiety and provide comfort.

2.7 Between requests for information from my spouse's attorney and my own attorney, I am totally overwhelmed. How do I manage gathering all of this detailed information by the deadlines imposed?

First, simply get started. Often, thinking about a task is worse than the job itself.

Second, break it down into smaller tasks. Perhaps one evening you gather your tax returns and on the weekend you work on your monthly living expenses.

Third, let in support. Ask that friend of yours who just loves numbers to come over for an evening with her calculator to help you get organized.

Finally, communicate with your lawyer. Your attorney or paralegal may be able to make your job easier by giving you suggestions or help. It may be that essential information can be provided now and the details submitted later.

2.8 I am so depressed about my divorce that I'm having difficulty getting out of bed in the morning to care for my children. What should I do?

See your health care provider. Feelings of depression are common during a divorce. You also want to make sure that you identify any physical health concerns.

Although feelings of sadness are common during a divorce, more serious depression means it's time to seek professional support.

Your health and your ability to care for your children are both essential. Follow through on recommendations by your health care professionals for therapy, medication, or other measures to improve your wellness.

2.9 Will taking prescribed medication to help treat my insomnia and depression hurt my case?

Not necessarily. Talk to your health care professional and follow their recommendations. Taking care of your health is of the utmost importance during this difficult time, and will serve your best interests as well as the best interests of your children. Inform your attorney of any medications that you are taking or treatment that you are seeking.

2.10 I know I need help to cope with the stress of the divorce, but I can't afford counseling. What can I do?

You are wise to recognize that divorce is a time for letting in support. You can explore a number of options, including:

- Meeting with a member of the clergy or lay chaplain
- Joining a divorce support group
- Turning to friends and family members
- Going to a therapist or divorce coach. If budget is a concern, contact a social agency that offers counseling services on a sliding-fee scale.

2.11 I'm the one who filed for divorce, but I still have loving feelings toward my spouse and feel sad about divorcing. Does this mean I should dismiss my divorce?

Strong feelings of caring about your spouse often persist after a divorce is filed. Whether or not to proceed with a divorce is a deeply personal decision. Although feelings can inform us of our thoughts, sometimes they can also cause us to not look clearly at everything there is to see in our situation.

Have you and your spouse participated in marriage counseling? Has your spouse refused to seek treatment for an addiction? Are you worried about the safety of you or your children if you remain in the marriage? Can you envision yourself as financially secure if you remain in this marriage? Is your spouse involved in another relationship?

The answers to these questions can help you get clear about whether to consider reconciliation. Talk to your therapist, divorce coach, or spiritual advisor to help determine the right path for you.

2.12 Will my attorney charge me for the time I spend talking about my feelings about my spouse and my divorce?

It depends. If you are paying your attorney by the hour, expect to be charged for the time your attorney spends talking with you. If your attorney is being paid a flat rate for handling your divorce, the time spent talking with you will be included in the fee.

Remember, however, that divorce lawyers are typically not mental health professionals or counselors. While talking about your feelings with your lawyer is inevitable to some extent, it is usually a better use of your resources to minimize the time you spend with your lawyer trying to work through your feelings about the divorce. Seek support instead from your support groups. (*See* question 2.10).

2.13 My attorney doesn't seem to realize how difficult my divorce is for me. How can I get him to understand?

Everyone wants support and compassion from the professionals who help during a divorce. Speak frankly with your attorney about your concerns. It may be that your lawyer does not see your concerns as being relevant to their job of getting your desired outcome in the divorce. Your willingness to improve the communication will help your lawyer understand how best to support you in the process and will help you understand which matters are best left for discussion with your therapist or a supportive friend.

2.14 I've been told not to speak ill of my spouse in front of my child, but I know she's doing this all the time. Why can't I just speak the truth?

It can be devastating for your child to hear you bad-mouthing his or her other parent. When a child hears a parent speak ill of the child's other parent, it will only make the child feel bad about himself or herself, as the child is part of both parents.

What your child needs is permission to love both of you, regardless of any bad parental behavior. The best way to support your child during this time is to encourage a positive relationship with the other parent.

2.15   Nobody in our family has ever been divorced and I feel really ashamed. Will my children feel the same way?

Making a change in how you see your family identity is huge for you. The best way to help your children is to establish a sense of pride in their new family and to look forward to the future with a real sense of possibility.

Your children will have an opportunity to witness you overcoming obstacles, demonstrating independence, and moving forward in your life, notwithstanding challenges. You can be a great teacher to them during this time by demonstrating pride in your family and in yourself.

2.16   I am very worried about having my deposition taken. My spouse's attorney is very aggressive, and I'm afraid I'm going to say something that will hurt my case.

A deposition is an opportunity for your spouse's attorney to gather information and to assess the type of witness you will be if the case proceeds to trial. Feeling anxious about your deposition is normal. However, regardless of the personality of the lawyers, most depositions in divorces are quite uneventful.

Remember that your attorney will be seated by your side at all times to support you. Ask to meet with your lawyer in advance to prepare for the deposition. If you are worried about certain questions that might be asked, talk to your attorney about them. Think of it as an opportunity, and enlist your lawyer's support in being well prepared.

2.17   I am still so angry at my spouse. How can I be expected to sit in the same room during a settlement conference or mediation?

If you are still really angry at your spouse, it may be beneficial to postpone the conference for a time. You might also consider seeking counseling to help you cope with your feelings of anger.

Another option might be "shuttle" negotiations. With this method, you and your attorney remain in one room while your spouse and his or her attorney are in another. Settlement offers are then relayed between the attorneys throughout the negotiation process. By shifting your focus from your angry feelings to your goal of a settlement, it may be easier to proceed through the process.

2.18   I'm afraid I can't make it through court without having an emotional breakdown. How do I prepare?

A divorce trial can be a highly emotional time, calling for a lot of support. Some of these ideas may help you through the process:

- Meet with your attorney or the firm's support staff in advance of your court date to prepare you for court.

- Ask you attorney whether there are any documents you should review in preparation for court, such as your deposition.

- Visit the courtroom in advance to get comfortable with the surroundings.

- Ask your attorney about having a support person with you on your court date.

- Ask yourself what is the worst thing that could happen and consider what options you would have if it did.

- Avoid alcohol, eat healthy, exercise, and get plenty of rest during the period of time leading up to the court date. Each of these will help you to prepare for the emotions of the day.

- Plan what you intend to wear in advance. Small preparations will lower your stress.

- Visualize the experience going well. Picture yourself sitting in the witness chair, giving clear, confident, and truthful answers to easy questions.

- Arrive early to the courthouse and make sure you have a plan for parking your car if you are not familiar with the area.

- Take slow, deep breaths. Breathing deeply will steady your voice, calm your nerves, and improve your focus.

By taking the above steps, you can make your court experience less stressful. Your attorney will be there to support you throughout the proceedings.

2.19   I am really confused. One day I think the divorce is a mistake. The next day I know I can't go back. A few minutes later I can hardly wait to be single again. Some days I just don't believe I'm getting divorced. What's happening?

Denial, transition, and acceptance are common passages for a person going through a divorce. One moment you might feel excited about your future and a few hours later you think your life is ruined.

What can be helpful to remember is that you may not pass from one stage to the next in a direct line. Feelings of anger or sadness may well up in you long after you thought you had moved on. Similarly, your mood might feel bright one day as you think about your future plans, even though you still miss your spouse.

Taking good care of yourself is essential during this period of your life. What you are going through requires a tremendous amount of energy. Allow yourself to experience your emotions, but also continue moving forward with your life. These steps will help your life get easier day by day.

3

Working with Your Attorney

If there is one thing you can be sure of in your divorce, it's that you will be given plenty of advice. Well-intentioned neighbors, cousins, and complete strangers will be happy to tell you war stories about their ex or about their sister who got divorced in Canada. Many will insist they know what you should do, even though they know nothing about the facts of your case or the law in Tennessee.

But there is one person whose advice will matter to you: your attorney. Your lawyer should be your trusted and supportive advocate at all times throughout your divorce. The counsel of your attorney can affect your life for years to come. You will never regret taking the time and energy to choose the right attorney for you.

See your relationship with your attorney as a partnership for pursuing what is most important to you. With clear and open attorney-client communication, you'll have the best outcome possible and your entire divorce will be less stressful.

By working closely with the right lawyer, you can trust the professional advice you receive and simply thank your cousin Millie for sharing.

3.1 Where do I begin looking for an attorney for my divorce?

There are many ways to find a divorce lawyer. Ask people you trust—friends and family members who have gone through a divorce, if they thought they had a good lawyer (or if their former spouse did!). If you know professionals who work with attorneys, ask for a referral to an attorney who is experienced in family law.

Go online. Most attorneys have websites that provide information on their practice areas, professional associations, experience, and philosophy.

3.2   How do I know if I am choosing the right attorney?

Choosing the right attorney for your divorce is an important decision. Your attorney should be a trusted professional with whom you feel comfortable sharing information openly. He or she should be a person you can trust and a zealous advocate for your interests.

You will rely upon your attorney to help you make many decisions throughout the course of your divorce. You will also entrust your legal counsel to make a range of strategic and procedural decisions on your behalf.

Consultation for a divorce might be your first meeting with a lawyer. Know that attorneys want to be supportive and to fully inform you. Feel free to seek all of the information you need to help you feel secure in knowing you have made the right choice.

Find an attorney who practices primarily in the family law area. Although many attorneys handle divorces, it is likely you will have more effective representation at a lower cost from an attorney who already knows the fundamentals of divorce law in Tennessee.

Determine the level of experience you want in your attorney. For example, if you have had a short marriage, have no children and few assets, an attorney with lesser experience might be a good value for your legal needs. However, if you are anticipating a custody dispute or have complex or substantial assets, a more experienced attorney may better meet your needs.

Consider the qualities in an attorney that are important to you. Even the most experienced and skilled attorney is not right for every person. Ask yourself what you are really looking for in an attorney so you can make your choice with these standards in mind.

It is important that you be confident in the attorney you hire. If you're unsure about whether the lawyer is really listening to you or understanding your concerns, keep looking until you find one who will. Your divorce is an important matter. It's critical that you have a professional you can trust.

3.3   Should I hire a "bulldog"—a very aggressive attorney?

Again, consider the qualities in an attorney that are important to you. A "bulldog" may promise to be overly aggressive and take your spouse for everything he or she is worth. However, it may be important to you to create a mutually respectful relationship with your spouse during and after the divorce, especially if there are minor children involved.

Additionally, expect the cost of your divorce to exponentially increase if your attorney is unwilling to negotiate and drags your spouse into court at every opportunity. Look for a lawyer who can represent you with zealous advocacy, while at the same time maintaining a high level of courtesy, professionalism, and integrity.

3.4   Should I interview more than one attorney?

Be willing to interview more than one attorney. Every lawyer has different strengths, and it is important that you find the one that is right for you. Sometimes it is only by meeting with more than one attorney that you see clearly who will best be able to help you reach your goals in the way you want. Changing lawyers in the middle of litigation can be stressful and costly. It is wise to invest energy at the outset in making the right choice.

3.5   My spouse says that since we're still friends, we should use the same attorney for the divorce. Is this a good idea?

Even the most amicable of divorcing couples usually have differing interests. For this reason, it is never recommended that an attorney represent both parties to a divorce. In most cases, an attorney is ethically prohibited from representing two people with conflicting interests who are in dispute.

Sometimes couples reach agreements without understanding all of their rights under the law. A client often will benefit from receiving further legal advice on matters such as tax considerations, retirement, and health insurance issues.

It is not uncommon for one party to retain an attorney and for the other party not to do so. In such cases, the party with the attorney files the complaint, and agreements reached between the parties are typically sent to the spouse for approval prior to any court hearing. If your spouse has filed for divorce and said that you do not need an attorney, you should nevertheless meet with a lawyer for advice on how proceeding without a lawyer could affect your legal rights.

3.6 I've been divorced before and I don't think I need an attorney this time. However, my spouse is hiring one. Is it wise to go it alone?

Having gone through a prior divorce, it's likely that you have learned a great deal about the divorce process as well as your legal rights. However, there are many reasons why you should be extremely cautious about proceeding without legal representation.

It is important to remember that every divorce is different. The length of the marriage, whether there are children, the relative financial situation for you and your spouse, as well as your age and health can all affect the financial outcome in your divorce.

The law may have changed since your last divorce. Some aspects of divorce law are likely to change each year. New laws get passed and new decisions get handed down regularly by the Tennessee Supreme Court and the Tennessee Court of Appeals that affect the rights and responsibilities of people who divorce.

In some cases, the involvement of your lawyer could be minimal. This might be the case if your marriage was short, your financial situation is very similar to that of your spouse, there are no children, and the two of you remain amicable. At a minimum, have an initial consultation with an attorney to discuss your rights and always have an attorney review any final agreement.

3.7 What information should I take with me to the first meeting with an attorney?

Attorneys differ on the amount of information they like to see at an initial consultation. If a court proceeding, either a divorce or a protection order, has already been initiated by either you or your spouse, it is important to take copies of any court documents.

If you and your spouse have a *prenuptial* or *postnuptial agreement*, a written agreement that directs how matters will be handled in the event of a divorce, that is another important document for you to bring at the outset of your case.

If you intend to ask for support, either for yourself or for your children, documents evidencing income of both you and your spouse will also be useful. These might include:

- Recent pay stubs
- Individual and business tax returns, W-2s, and 1099s
- Bank statements showing deposits
- A statement of your monthly budget

If your situation is urgent or you do not have access to these documents, don't let it stop you from scheduling your appointment with an attorney. Prompt legal advice about your rights is often more important than having detailed financial information in the beginning. Your attorney can explain to you the options for obtaining these financial records if they are not readily available to you.

Your attorney will ask you to complete a questionnaire at your first meeting. Ask whether it is possible to do this in advance of your meeting. This can allow you to provide more complete information and to make the most of your appointment time with the lawyer.

3.8 What unfamiliar words might an attorney use at the first meeting?

Law has a language all its own, and attorneys sometimes lapse into "legalese," forgetting non-attorneys may not recognize words used daily in the practice of law. Some words and phrases you might hear include:

- *Dissolution of marriage*—the divorce

- *Petitioner*—person who files the divorce complaint
- *Respondent*—person who did not file the divorce complaint
- *Jurisdiction*—authority of a court to make rulings affecting a party
- *Service*—process of notifying a party about a legal filing
- *Discovery*—process during which each side provides information to each other
- *Decree*—the final order entered in a divorce

Never hesitate to ask your attorney the meaning of a term. Your complete understanding of your attorney's advice is essential for you to partner with your advocate as effectively as possible.

3.9   What can I expect at an initial consultation with an attorney?

Most attorneys will ask that you complete a questionnaire prior to the meeting. With few exceptions, attorneys are required to keep confidential all information you provide.

The nature of the advice you get from an attorney in an initial consultation will depend upon whether you are still deciding whether you want a divorce, whether you are planning for a possible divorce in the future, or whether you are ready to file for divorce right away.

During the meeting, you will have an opportunity to provide the following information to the attorney:

- A brief history of your marriage
- Background information regarding yourself, your spouse, and your children
- Your immediate situation
- Your intentions and goals regarding your relationship with your spouse
- What information you are seeking from the attorney during the consultation

You can expect the attorney to provide the following information to you:

- The procedure for divorce in Tennessee
- Identification of important issues in your case
- A preliminary assessment of your rights and responsibilities under the law
- Background information regarding the firm
- Information about fees and filings

Although some questions may be impossible for the attorney to answer at the initial consultation because additional information or research is needed, the initial consultation is an opportunity for you to ask all of the questions you have at the time of the meeting.

3.10   Will all communication with my attorney be confidential?

Yes. Your lawyer has an ethical duty to maintain your confidentiality. This duty of confidentiality also extends to the legal staff working with your attorney. The privileged information that you share with your attorney will remain private and confidential, unless such privilege is waived by your voluntarily disclosing it to third parties.

3.11   Is there any way I could inadvertently waive the attorney-client privilege as it relates to the duty of confidentiality?

Yes. To ensure that communications between you and your attorney remain confidential, and to protect against the voluntary or involuntary waiver of such privilege, below are some tips to consider:

- Refrain from disclosing the content of the communications with your attorney, or discussing in substantive detail the communications with your attorney, with third parties. Third parties include friends and family members.

- Social media provides the potential for waiving the attorney-client privilege by your publicly disclosing confidential information. Do not post information or send messages relating to your case on Facebook, Twitter, or other social media websites.

- Do not post information relating to your case or communications with your attorney on a personal blog, video blog, online chat rooms, or online message boards.

- Depending upon your employer's policy regarding electronic communication, the attorney-client privilege may be waived by communicating with your attorney or by discussing your case through your personal e-mail account (Gmail, Yahoo, etc.) via a company computer. To ensure your communications remain confidential, it is best to only communicate via e-mail from your private e-mail address from your home computer.

3.12 Can I take a friend or family member to my initial consultation?

Yes. Having someone present during your initial consultation can be a source of great support. You might ask him or her to take notes on your behalf so that you can focus on listening and asking questions. Remember that this is your consultation, however, and it is important that the attorney hears the facts of your case directly from you. Also, ask your attorney how having a third party present at your consultation could impact the attorney-client privilege.

3.13 What exactly will my attorney do to help me get a divorce?

Your attorney will play a critical role in helping to obtain your divorce. You will be actively involved in some of the work, but other actions will be taken by your lawyer behind the scenes at the law office, a law library, or the courthouse.

Your attorney may perform any of the following tasks on your behalf:

- Assess the case to determine which court has jurisdiction to hear your divorce

- Develop a strategy for advising you about all aspects of your divorce, including the treatment of assets and matters concerning children

- Prepare legal documents for filing with the court

- Conduct discovery to obtain information from the other party, which could include depositions, requests for production of documents, and written interrogatories
- Appear with you at all court appearances, depositions, and conferences.
- Schedule all deadlines and court appearances
- Support you in responding to information requests from your spouse
- Inform you of actions you are required to take
- Perform financial analyses of your case
- Conduct legal research
- Prepare you for court appearances and depositions
- Prepare your case for hearings and trial, including preparing exhibits and interviewing witnesses
- Advise you regarding your rights under the law
- Counsel you regarding the risks and benefits of negotiated settlement as compared to proceeding to trial

As your advocate, your attorney is entrusted to take all steps necessary to represent your interests in the divorce.

3.14 What professionals should I expect to work with during my divorce?

Depending upon the issues identified by your attorney, you can expect to work with various types of professionals, such as appraisers, financial professionals, real estate agents, and mental health experts.

Additionally, in some cases where custody or parenting time issues are seriously disputed, the court may appoint a *guardian ad litem (GAL)*. This person, usually a lawyer, has the duty to represent the best interests of the child. A guardian *ad litem* has the responsibility to investigate you and your spouse as well as the needs of your child. She or he may then be called as a witness at trial to testify regarding any relevant observations.

Another expert who could be appointed by the court is a psychologist. The role of the psychologist will depend upon the purpose for which she or he is appointed. For example, the psychologist may be appointed to perform a child-custody evaluation, which involves assessing both parents and the child, or this expert may be ordered to evaluate one parent to assess the child's safety while spending time with that parent.

3.15   Can I bring my children to meetings with my attorney?

It's best to make other arrangements for your children when you meet with your attorney. Your attorney will be giving you a great deal of important information during your conferences, and it will benefit you to give your full attention. It's also recommended that you take every measure to keep information about the legal aspects of your divorce away from your children. Knowledge that you are seeing an attorney can add to your child's anxiety about the process. It can also make your child a target for questioning by the other parent about your contacts with your attorney.

Most law offices are not designed to accommodate young children and are ordinarily not "child-proof." For both your child's well-being and your own peace of mind, explore options for someone to care for your child when you have meetings with your attorney.

3.16   What is the role of the *paralegal* or *legal assistant* in my attorney's office?

A *paralegal,* or *legal assistant,* is a trained legal professional whose duties include providing support for you and your lawyer. Working with a paralegal can make your divorce easier because he or she is likely to be very available to help you. It can also lower your legal costs, as the hourly rate for paralegal services is less than the rate for attorneys.

A paralegal is prohibited from giving legal advice. It is important that you respect the limits of the role of the paralegal if he or she is unable to answer your question because it calls for giving a legal opinion. However, a paralegal can answer many questions and provide a great deal of information to you throughout your divorce.

Paralegals can help you by receiving information from you, reviewing documents with you, providing you with updates on your case, and answering questions about the divorce process that do not call for legal advice.

3.17 My attorney is not returning my phone calls. What can I do?

You have a right to expect your phone calls to be returned by your attorney. Here are some options to consider:

- Ask to speak to the paralegal or another attorney in the office.

- Send an e-mail or fax telling your attorney that you have been trying to reach him or her by phone and explaining the reason it is important that you receive a call back.

- Ask the receptionist to schedule a phone conference for you to speak with your attorney at a specific date and time.

- Schedule a meeting with your attorney to discuss both the issue needing attention as well as your concerns about the poor communication.

Your attorney wants to provide good service to you. If your calls are not being returned, take action to get the communication with your attorney back on track.

3.18 How do I know when it's time to change attorneys?

Changing lawyers is costly. You will incur legal fees for your new attorney to review information that is already familiar to the attorney you are leaving. You will spend time giving much of the same information to your new lawyer that you gave to the one you have discharged. A change in lawyers also often results in delays in the divorce.

The following are questions to ask yourself when you're deciding whether to stay with your attorney or seek new counsel:

- Have I spoken directly to my attorney about my concerns?

- When I expressed concerns, did my attorney take action accordingly?

- Is my attorney open and receptive to what I have to say?

- Am I blaming my attorney for the bad behavior of my spouse or opposing counsel?

- Have I provided my attorney the information needed for taking the next action?

- Does my attorney have control over the complaints I have, or are they ruled by the law or the judge?

- Is my attorney keeping promises for completing actions in my case?

- Do I trust my attorney?

- What would be the advantages of changing lawyers when compared to the cost?

- Do I believe my attorney will support me to achieve the outcome I'm seeking in my divorce?

Every effort should be made to resolve your concerns about your attorney. If you have made this effort and the situation remains unchanged, the it may be time to switch lawyers.

3.19 Are there certain expectations that I should have when working with my legal team?

Yes. Your attorney will guide you throughout the divorce process. There are certain actions you can expect your lawyer to take for you during your divorce. A list of some of them follows.

Meet with you prior to the filing of a court action to advise you on actions you should take first. There may be important steps to take before you initiate the legal process. Your attorney can support you to be well prepared prior to initiating divorce.

Take action to obtain a temporary court order or to enforce existing orders. Temporary court orders are often needed to ensure clarity regarding rights and responsibilities while your divorce is pending. Your attorney can help you obtain a temporary order and ask the court to enforce its orders if there is a violation.

Explain the legal process during each step of your case. Understanding the legal process reduces the stress of your divorce. Your attorney can guide you each step of the way.

Listen to your concerns and answer any legal questions. Your attorney can give you advice on legal matters and direct you to the right person who can help with many of your other concerns.

Support you in developing your parenting plan. Many parents do not know how to decide what type of parenting plan is best for their children. Your attorney can help you look at the needs of you children and offer advice based on his or her experience in working with families.

Support you in the completion of your discovery responses and preparing for depositions. The discovery process can be overwhelming for anyone. You will be asked to provide detailed information and many documents. Your attorney can make this job easier. Just ask. If your case involves depositions, your attorney will support you to be fully prepared for the experience.

Identify important issues, analyze the evidence, and advise you. Divorce is complex. Often, there is a great deal of uncertainty. Your lawyer can analyze the unique facts of your case and advise you based upon the law.

Communicate with the opposing party's attorney to try to resolve issues without going to court, and to keep your case progressing. Although your attorney cannot control the actions of the opposing party or their lawyer, your lawyer can always initiate communication as your advocate. Phoning, e-mailing, or writing to opposing counsel are actions your attorney can take to encourage cooperation and to keep your divorce moving forward at the pace you want without the expense of contested litigation.

Think creatively regarding challenges with your case and provide options for your consideration. At the outset, you may see many obstacles to reaching a final resolution. Your lawyer can offer creative ideas for resolving challenges and help you to explore your options to achieve the best possible outcome.

Facilitate the settlement process. Although your attorney can never make the other party settle, he or she can take action to promote settlement. Your lawyer can prepare settlement proposals, invite settlement conferences, and negotiate zealously on your behalf.

3.20   Are there certain things my legal team will not be able to do?

Yes. Although there are many ways in which your lawyer can support you during your divorce, there are also things he or she will not be able to accomplish. Following are some of these.

Force the other parent to exercise their parenting time. Your attorney cannot force a parent to exercise parenting time. However, be mindful that a chronic neglect of parenting time may be a basis for modifying your parenting plan. Tell your attorney if the other parent is repeatedly failing to exercise their parenting time.

Force the other party to respond to a settlement proposal. Your attorney may send proposals or make requests to opposing counsel; however, there is no duty to respond. After repeated follow-ups without a response, it may be clear no response is coming. At that time, your attorney will decide whether the issues merit court action. Both parties must agree on all terms for a case to be settled without a trial. If one party wants to proceed to trial, even over a single issue, he/she will be able to do so.

Control the tone of communication from opposing counsel or communications from the other party, or the other party's family members. Unfortunately, communication from the opposing attorney may sometimes appear rude, condescending, or demanding. Your lawyer cannot stop an attorney from using these tactics.

Absent a pattern of harassment, your attorney cannot stop the other party or third parties from contacting you. If you do not want the contact, talk with your attorney about how to best handle the situation. Of course, appropriate communication regarding your children is always encouraged.

Ask the court to compensate you for every wrong done to you by the other party over the course of your marriage. Although your attorney will empathize that you do have valid complaints, understand that focusing on the most important issues will yield the best outcome in the end. Raising numerous small issues may distract from your most important goals.

Remedy poor financial decisions made during the marriage. With few exceptions, the court's duty is to divide the marital estate as it currently exists. The judge will not attempt to remedy all past financial wrongs, such as overspending or poor investments by your spouse. If there is significant debt, consult with a debt counselor or bankruptcy lawyer.

Control how the other party parents your children during his/her parenting time. Each parent has strengths and weaknesses. Absent special needs of a child, most judges will not issue orders regarding bedtimes, amount of TV watching or playing video games, discipline methods, clothing, or diet. Of course, any suspected abuse should be reported immediately to the appropriate authorities.

Demand an accounting of how a parent uses court-ordered child support. Absent extraordinary circumstances, the court will not order the other parent to provide an accounting for the use of child support.

Leverage money for rights regarding your children. Tactics oriented toward asserting custody rights as leverage toward attaining financial goals will be discouraged. Your attorney should negotiate parenting issues based solely on considerations related to your child, then separately negotiate child support based on financial considerations.

Guarantee payment of child support and alimony. Enforcement of payment of support is only possible when it is court ordered. However, even with a court order, you may experience inconsistent timing of payments due to job loss or a refusal to pay. Talk with your attorney if a pattern of repeated missed payments has developed.

Collect child care and uninsured medical expenses if provisions of the decree are not complied with. If your decree requires you to provide documentation of payment of expenses to the other party and you fail to do so, you could be prohibited from collecting reimbursement for those expenses. Follow the court's orders regarding providing documentation to the other parent, even if they don't pay as they should. Always keep records of these expenses and payments made by each parent, and keep copies of communications with the other parent regarding payment/reimbursement. It is much easier to keep these records on an ongoing basis than to get copies of old checks, day care bills, medical bills, and insurance documents at a later time.

4

Attorney Fees and Costs

A ny time you make a major investment, you want to know what the cost is going to be and what you are getting for your money. Investing in quality legal representation for your divorce is no different.

The cost of your divorce might be one of your greatest concerns. Because of this, you will want to be an intelligent consumer of legal services. You want quality, but you also want to get the best value for the fees you are paying.

Legal fees for a divorce can be costly and the total expense not always predictable. But there are many actions you can take to control and estimate the cost. Develop a plan early on for how you will finance your divorce. Speak openly with your lawyer about fees from the outset. Learn as much as you can about how you will be charged. Insist on a written fee agreement.

By being informed, aware, and wise, your financial investment in your divorce will be money well spent to protect your future.

4.1 Can I get free legal advice from an attorney over the phone?

Every law firm has its own policy regarding lawyers talking to people who are not yet clients of the firm. Most questions about your divorce are too complex for a lawyer to give a meaningful answer during a brief phone call.

Questions about your divorce require a complete look at the facts, circumstances, and background of your marriage.

To obtain good legal advice, it's best to schedule an initial consultation with a lawyer who handles divorces.

4.2 Will I be charged for an initial consultation with an attorney?

It depends. Some lawyers give free consultations, while some charge a fee. When scheduling your appointment, you should be told the amount of the fee. Payment is ordinarily due at the time of the consultation.

4.3 If I decide to hire an attorney, when do I have to pay him or her?

If your attorney charges for an initial consultation, be prepared to make payment at the time of your meeting. At the close of your consultation, the attorney may tell you the amount of the retainer needed by the law firm to handle your divorce. However, you are not obligated to pay the retainer at the time of your first meeting. Rather, the retainer is paid after you have decided to hire the lawyer, the lawyer has accepted your case, and you are ready to proceed.

4.4 How much does it cost to get a divorce?

The cost of your divorce will depend upon many factors. Some attorneys perform divorces for a flat fee, but most charge by the hour. A *flat fee* is a fixed amount for the legal services being provided. A flat fee is more likely to be used when there are no children of the marriage and the parties have agreed upon the division of their property and debts. Most Tennessee attorneys charge by the hour for divorces.

It is important that you discuss the cost of your divorce at your first meeting with your attorney. It is customary for family law attorneys to request a retainer, also known as a fee advance, prior to beginning work on your case.

Be sure to ask your attorney what portion, if any, of the retainer is refundable if you do not continue with the case or if you terminate your relationship with the attorney.

4.5 What exactly is a *retainer* and how much can I expect mine to be?

A *retainer* is a sum paid to your lawyer in advance for services to be performed and costs to be incurred in your divorce. This will be either an amount paid toward a "flat fee" for your divorce, or an advance credit for services that will be charged by the hour.

If your case is accepted by the law firm, expect the attorney to request a retainer following the initial consultation. The amount of the retainer may be several thousand dollars, depending upon the nature of your case. Contested custody, divorces involving businesses or interstate disputes, for example, are all likely to require higher retainers.

Other factors that can affect the amount of the retainer include the nature and number of the disputed issues.

4.6 Will my attorney accept my divorce case on a contingency fee basis?

No. A contingency fee is one that only becomes payable if your case is successful. In Tennessee, lawyers are prohibited from entering into a contingency fee contract in any divorce case. Your lawyer may not accept payment based upon securing your divorce, the amount of alimony or support awarded, or the division of the property settlement.

4.7 What are typical hourly rates for a divorce attorney?

In Tennessee, attorneys who practice in the divorce area charge from $200 per hour to more than twice that rate. The rate your attorney charges may depend upon factors such as his or her skills, reputation, experience, exclusive focus on divorce law, and what other attorneys in the area are charging.

If you have a concern about the amount of an attorney's hourly rate, but you would like to hire the firm with which the attorney is associated, consider asking to work with an associate attorney in the firm who is likely to charge a lower rate. Associates are attorneys who ordinarily have less experience than the senior partners. However, they often are trained by the senior partners, are very experienced, and are fully capable of handling your case.

4.8   If I can't afford to pay the full amount of the retainer, can I make monthly payments to my attorney?

Every law firm has its own policies regarding payment arrangements for divorce clients. Often, these arrangements are tailored to the specific client. Most attorneys will require a substantial retainer to be paid at the outset of your case. Some attorneys may accept monthly payments in lieu of the retainer. Most will require monthly payments in addition to the initial retainer, or request additional retainers as your case progresses. Ask frank questions of your attorney to have clarity about your responsibility for payment of legal fees.

4.9   I agreed to pay my attorney a substantial retainer to begin my case. Will I still have to make monthly payments?

Ask your attorney at your first meeting what will be expected of you regarding payments on your account while the divorce is in progress. Clarify whether monthly payments on your account will be expected, whether it is likely that you will be asked to pay additional retainers, and whether the firm charges interest on past-due accounts. Regular payments to your attorney can help you avoid having a tremendously burdensome legal bill at the end of your case. Additionally, you may also be required to keep a minimum credit balance on your account to ensure your case is adequately funded for ongoing work by your attorney.

4.10   How will I know how the fees and charges are accumulating?

Periodically, you may ask your attorney to send you statements regarding how much of your retainer fee has been used. This will allow you to plan for further expenses as your case progresses. Talk with your attorney during your meetings regarding the status of your account.

4.11   What other expenses are related to the divorce litigation besides attorney fees?

Talk to your attorney about costs other than the attorney fees. Ask whether it is likely there will be filing fees, court reporter expenses, subpoenas, expert-witness fees, mediation, or parenting class fees. Expert-witness fees can be a substantial expense, ranging from hundreds to thousands of dollars, depending upon the type of expert and the extent to which he or she is involved in your case.

Speak frankly with your attorney about these costs so that together you can make the best decisions about how to use your budget for the litigation.

4.12 Who pays for the services of experts such as appraisers, accountants, psychologists, and mediators?

Costs for the services of experts, whether appointed by the court or hired by the parties, are ordinarily paid for by the parties.

In the case of the guardian *ad litem,* who may be appointed to represent the best interests of your children, the amount of the fee will depend upon how much time this professional spends. The judge often orders this fee to be shared by the parties. However, depending upon the circumstances, one party can be ordered to pay the entire fee.

Psychologists either charge by the hour or set a flat fee for a certain type of evaluation. Again, the court can order one party to pay this fee or both parties to share the expense. It is not uncommon for a psychologist to request payment in advance and hold the release of an expert report until fees are paid.

Mediators either charge a flat fee per session or an hourly rate fee. Generally, each party will pay one-half of the mediator's fee, which is paid prior to your mediation sessions.

The fees for many experts, including appraisers and accountants, will vary depending upon whether the individuals are called upon to provide only a specific service such as an appraisal, or whether they will need to prepare for giving testimony and appear as a witness at trial.

4.13 What factors will impact how much my divorce will cost?

Although it is often difficult to predict how much your legal fees will be, the following are some of the factors that affect the cost:

- Whether there are children
- Whether child custody is agreed upon
- Whether there are novel legal questions
- Whether a pension plan will be divided between the parties
- The nature of the issues contested
- The number of issues agreed to by the parties
- The cooperation of the opposing party and opposing counsel
- The frequency of your communication with your legal team
- The ability of the parties to communicate with each other, as well as the client's ability to communicate with his or her attorney
- The promptness with which information is provided and/or exchanged between both the clients and the attorneys
- Whether there are litigation costs, such as fees for expert witnesses or court reporters
- The hourly rate of the attorney
- The time it will take to conclude your divorce

Communicating with your attorney regularly about your legal fees will help you to have a better understanding of the overall cost as your case proceeds.

4.14 Will my attorney charge for phone calls and e-mails?

Unless your case is being handled on a flat-fee basis, you should expect to be billed for any communication with your attorney. Many of the professional services provided by lawyers are done by phone and by e-mail. This time can be spent giving legal advice, negotiating, or gathering information to protect your interests. These calls and e-mails are all legal services for which you should anticipate being charged by your attorney.

To make the most of your time during attorney phone calls, plan your call in advance. Organize the information you want to relay, your questions, and any concerns to be addressed. This will help you to be clear and focused during the phone call so that your fees are well spent.

4.15 Will I be charged for talking to the staff at my attorney's office?

It depends. Check the terms of your fee agreement with your lawyer. Whether you are charged fees for talking to non-lawyer members of the law office may depend upon their role in the office. For example, many law firms charge for the services of paralegals and law clerks.

Remember that nonlawyers cannot give legal advice, so it is important to respect their roles. Don't expect the receptionist to give you an opinion regarding whether you will win custody or receive alimony.

Your lawyer's support staff will be able relay your messages and receive information from you. They may also be able to answer many of your questions. Allowing this type of support from within the firm is an important way to control your legal fees, too.

4.16 How do I know whether I should spend the attorney fees my lawyer says it will require to take my case to trial?

Deciding whether to take a case to trial or to settle is often the most challenging point in the divorce process. This decision should be made with the support of your attorney.

When the issues in dispute are primarily financial, often the decision about settlement is related to the costs of going to trial. Get clear about just how far apart you and your spouse are on the financial matters and compare this to the estimated costs of going to trial. By comparing these amounts, you can decide whether a compromise on certain financial issues and certainty about the outcome would be better than paying legal fees and not knowing how your case will resolve.

4.17 Is there any way I can reduce some of the expenses of getting a divorce?

Litigation of any kind can be expensive, and divorces are no exception. The good news is that there are many ways that you can help control the expense. Here are some of them:

Put it in writing. If you need to relay information that is important but not urgent, consider providing it to your attorney by mail, fax, or e-mail. This creates a prompt and accurate record for your file and takes less time than exchanging phone messages and talking on the phone.

Keep your attorney informed. Just as your attorney should keep you up to date on the status of your case, you need to do the same. Keep your attorney advised about any major developments in your life, such as plans to move, have someone move into your home, change in your employment status, or buy or sell significant property. During your divorce, if your contact information changes, be sure to notify your attorney.

Obtain copies of documents. An important part of litigation includes reviewing documents such as tax returns, account statements, report cards, or medical records. Your attorney will ordinarily be able to request or subpoena these items, but many of them may be readily available to you directly upon request. The more you can do yourself, the less your fees will be. Always ensure the information is presented to your attorney neatly and organized. If your attorney has to sort through items thrown into a box, your fees may be greater than if you had done nothing at all.

Consult your attorney's website. If your attorney has a website, it may be a great source of useful information. The answers to commonly asked questions about the divorce process can often be found there.

Utilize support professionals. Get to know the support staff at your attorney's office. Although only attorneys are able to give you legal advice, the receptionist, paralegal, legal secretary, or law clerk may be able to answer your questions regarding the status of your case. All communication with any professionals in a law firm is required to be kept strictly confidential.

Consider working with an associate attorney. Although the senior attorneys or partners in a law firm may have more experience, you may find that working with an associate attorney is a good option. Hourly rates for an associate attorney are sometimes lower than those charged by a senior partner and the associate may be more available to assist you, particularly if the senior partner is in a trial. Frequently, the associate attorney has trained under a senior partner and developed excellent legal.

Leave a detailed message. If your attorney knows the information you are seeking, she or he can often get the answer before returning your call. This not only gets your answer faster, but also reduces costs.

Discuss more than one matter during a call. It is not unusual for clients to have many questions during litigation. If your question is not urgent, consider waiting to call until you have more than one inquiry. However, never hesitate to call to ask any legal question.

Provide timely responses to information requests. Whenever possible, provide information requested by your attorney in a timely manner. This avoids the cost of follow-up action by your attorney and the additional expense of extending the time in litigation.

Carefully review your monthly statements. Scrutinize your monthly billing statements closely. If you believe an error has been made, contact your attorney's office right away to discuss your concerns. Your attorney will want to make things right.

Remain open to settlement. Understand that when your disagreement concerns financial matters, the amount of money in dispute may be less than the amount it will cost to go to trial.

By doing your part, you can use your legal fees wisely and control the costs of your divorce.

4.18　I don't have much money, but I need to get a divorce as quickly as possible. What should I do?

If you have some money and want to obtain a divorce as soon as possible, consider some of these options:

- Borrow the legal fees from friends or family. Often those close to you are concerned about your future and would be pleased to support you in your goal of having your rights protected. Although asking for a loan may be uncomfortable to do, remember that most family members and friends will appreciate that you trusted them enough to ask for their help. If the retainer is too much money to request from a single individual, consider whether a handful of persons might each be able to contribute a lesser amount to enable you to hire a lawyer.

- Charge the legal fees on a low-interest credit card or consider taking out a loan.
- Start saving. If your case is not urgent, consider developing a plan for saving the money you need to proceed with a divorce. Your attorney may be willing to receive and hold monthly payments until you have paid an amount sufficient to pay the initial retainer.
- Talk to your attorney about using money held in a joint account with your spouse.
- Find an attorney who will work with you on a monthly payment basis.
- Ask your attorney about your spouse paying for your legal fees
- Ask your attorney about being paid from the proceeds of the property settlement. If you and your spouse have acquired substantial assets during the marriage, you may be able to find an attorney who will wait to be paid until the assets are divided at the conclusion of the divorce.
- Closely examine all sources of funds readily available to you, as you may have overlooked money that might be easily accessible to you.

Even if you do not have the financial resources to proceed with your divorce at this time, consult with an attorney to learn your rights and to develop an action plan for steps you can take between now and the time you are able to proceed.

Often, there are measures you can take right away to protect yourself until you have the money to proceed with your divorce.

4.19 Is there anything I can do on my own to get support for my children if I don't have money for an attorney for a divorce?

Each judicial district in Tennessee has a child-support office through the district attorney's office in that district. You should consult with the assistant district attorney who handles child support for that office to determine the best method to start support.

4.20 If my mother pays my legal fees, will my attorney give her private information about my divorce?

If someone else is paying your legal fees, discuss with your attorney and the payor your expectations that your attorney will honor the ethical duty of confidentiality. Without your permission, your attorney should not disclose information to others about your case. However, if you authorize your attorney to speak with your family members, be aware that you will be charged for these communications. Regardless of the opinions of the person who pays your attorney fees, your attorney's duty is to remain *your* zealous advocate.

4.21 Can I ask the court to order my spouse to pay my attorney fees?

Yes. If you want to ask the court to order your spouse to pay any portion of your legal fees, be sure to discuss this with your attorney at the first opportunity. Most attorneys will treat the obligation for your legal fees as yours until the other party has made payment.

If your case is likely to require costly experts and your spouse has a much greater ability to pay these expenses, talk to your attorney about the possibility of filing a motion with the court asking your spouse to pay toward these costs while the case is pending.

4.22 What happens if I don't pay my attorney the fees I promised to pay?

The ethical rules for lawyers allow your attorney to withdraw from representation if you do not comply with your fee agreement. Your attorney may also file an attorney's lien against any judgment awarded to you to pay any outstanding attorney's fees or costs to the firm. Consequently, it is important that you keep the promises you have made regarding your account.

If you are having difficulty paying your attorney's fees, talk with your attorney about payment options. Consider borrowing the funds, using your credit card, or asking for help from friends and family.

Above all, do not avoid communication with your attorney if you are having challenges making payment. Keeping in touch with your attorney is essential for you to have an advocate at all stages of your divorce.

5

The Discovery Process

Discovery is one of the least talked about steps in divorce, but it is often among the most important. The purpose of discovery is to ensure that both you and your spouse have access to the same information and to fulfill the duty of full disclosure. In this way, you can either negotiate a fair agreement or have all of the facts and documents to present to the judge at trial. The discovery process enables you and your spouse to meet on a more level playing field when it comes to settling your case or taking it to trial. You and your spouse both need the same information if you hope to reach agreement on any of the issues in your divorce. Similarly, the judge must know all of the facts to make a fair decision.

The discovery process may seem tedious at times because of the need to obtain and to provide lots of detailed information. Completing it, however, can give tremendous clarity about the issues in your divorce. Trust your lawyer's advice about the importance of having the necessary evidence as you complete the discovery process in order to reach your goals in your divorce.

5.1   What is the legal definition of *discovery*?

Discovery is the part of your divorce process in which the attorneys attempt to learn as much about the facts of your case as possible. Through a variety of methods, both attorneys will request information from you, your spouse, and potential witnesses in your case.

5.2 What types of discovery might be done by my attorney or my spouse's attorney?

Types of discovery include:

- *Interrogatories*—which are written questions that must be answered under oath
- *Requests for production of documents*—which asks for certain documents to be provided by you or your spouse
- *Requests for admissions*—which asks for certain facts to be admitted or denied
- *Subpoena of documents*
- *Depositions*—in which questions are asked and answered under oath in the presence of a court reporter, but outside the presence of a judge

Factors that can influence the type of discovery conducted in your divorce can include:

- The types of issues in dispute
- How much access you and your spouse have to needed information
- The level of cooperation in sharing information
- The budget available for performing discovery

Talk to your attorney about the nature and extent of discovery anticipated in your case.

5.3 How long does the discovery process take?

Discovery can take anywhere from a few weeks to a number of months, depending upon the complexity of the case, the cooperation of you and your spouse, and whether expert witnesses are involved.

The Tennessee Rules of Civil Procedure provide that interrogatories, requests for production of documents, and requests for admissions be responded to within thirty days.

5.4   My attorney insists that we conduct discovery, but I don't want to spend the time and money on it. Is it really necessary?

The discovery process can be critical to a successful outcome in your case for several reasons:

- It increases the likelihood that any agreements reached are based on full and accurate information
- It provides necessary information for deciding whether to settle or proceed to trial
- It supports the preparation of defenses by providing information regarding your spouse's care.
- It avoids surprises at trial, such as unexpected witness testimony.
- It ensures all potential issues are identified by your attorney.

Discuss with your attorney the intention behind the discovery being conducted in your case to ensure it is consistent with your goals and a meaningful investment of your legal fees.

5.5   I just received from my spouse's attorney interrogatories and requests that I produce documents. My attorney wants me to respond within two weeks. I'll never make the deadline. What can I do?

Answering your discovery promptly will help move your case forward and help control your legal fees. There are steps you can take to make this task easier. First, look at all of the questions. Many of them will not apply or your answers will be a simple "yes" or "no."

Ask a friend or family member to help you. It is important to develop the practice of letting others help you while you are going through your divorce. Chances are that you will make great progress in just a couple of hours with help.

Break it down into smaller tasks. If you answer a few questions a day, the task will not be so overwhelming. Also, call your attorney. Ask whether a paralegal in the office can help you organize the needed information or determine whether some of it can be provided at a later date.

Delay in the discovery process often leads to frustration by clients and attorneys. Do your best to provide the information in a timely manner with the help of others.

5.6   I don't have access to my documents and my spouse is being uncooperative in providing my attorney with information. Can my attorney request information directly from an employer or financial institution?

Yes, it may be possible to issue a subpoena directly to an employer or financial institution. A *subpoena* is a court order directing an individual or corporate representative to appear before the court or to produce documents in a pending lawsuit. In the discovery process, a subpoena is used to require an individual or corporation to produce papers, books, or other physical documents that constitute or contain evidence relevant to your case.

5.7   My spouse's attorney intends to subpoena my medical records. Aren't these private?

Whether or not your medical records are relevant in your case will depend upon the issues in dispute. If you are requesting alimony or if your health is an issue in the dispute of child custody, these records may be relevant.

Talk with your lawyer about your rights. There are a number of options that may be available to prevent the disclosure of your medical information.

5.8   I own my business; will I have to disclose my business records?

Yes, you may be required to provide extensive records of your business in the discovery process. However, it is common for the court to protect the confidentiality of these records.

5.9   It's been two months since my attorney sent interrogatories to my spouse, and we still don't have his answers. I answered mine on time. Is there anything that can be done to speed up the process?

The failure or refusal of a spouse to follow the rules of discovery can add to both the frustration and expense of the divorce process. Talk with your attorney about filing a *motion to compel,* seeking a court order that your spouse must provide the requested information by a certain date. A request for attorney fees for the filing of the motion may also be appropriate.

Ask your lawyer whether a subpoena of information from an employer or a financial institution would be a more cost-effective way to get needed facts and documents if your spouse remains uncooperative.

5.10   What is a *deposition*?

A *deposition* is the asking and answering of questions under oath, outside of court, in the presence of a court reporter. A deposition may be taken of you, your spouse, or potential witnesses in your divorce case, including experts. Both attorneys will be present. You and your spouse also have the right to be present when depositions are taken of any witnesses in your case.

Depositions are not performed in every divorce. They are most common in cases involving contested custody, complex financial issues, and expert witnesses.

After your deposition is completed, the questions and answers will be transcribed, that is, typed by the court reporter exactly as given.

5.11   What is the purpose of a deposition?

A deposition can serve a number of purposes such as:

- Supporting the settlement process by providing valuable information
- Helping your attorney determine which witnesses to use at trial
- Aiding in the assessment of a witness's credibility, that is, whether the witness appears to be telling the truth
- Helping avoid surprises at the trial by learning the testimony of witnesses in advance
- Preserving testimony in the event the witness becomes unavailable for trial

Depositions can be essential tools in a divorce, especially when a case is likely to proceed to trial.

5.12 Will what I say in my deposition be used against me when we go to court?

Usually, a deposition is used to develop trial strategy and obtain information in preparation for trial. In some circumstances, a deposition may be used at trial.

If you are called later to testify as a witness and you give testimony contrary to your deposition, your deposition can be used to impeach you by showing the inconsistency in your statements. This could cause you to lose credibility with the court. It is important to review your deposition prior to your live testimony at trial to ensure consistency and prepare yourself for the type of questions you may be asked.

5.13 Will the judge read the depositions?

Unless a witness becomes unavailable for trial or gives conflicting testimony at trial, it is unlikely that the judge will ever read the depositions.

5.14 How should I prepare for my deposition?

To prepare for your deposition, review the important documents in your case, such as the complaint, your answers to interrogatories, your financial affidavit, and any temporary hearing affidavits.

Gather all documents you've been asked to provide at your deposition. Deliver them to your attorney in advance of your deposition for copying and review. Talk to your attorney about the type of questions you can expect to be asked. Discuss with him or her any questions you are concerned about answering.

5.15 What will I be asked? Can I refuse to answer questions?

Questions in a deposition can cover a broad range of topics, from your personal relationships to your marital property. The attorney is allowed to ask anything that is reasonably calculated to lead to the discovery of admissible evidence. If the question may lead to relevant information, it can be asked in a deposition, even though it may be inadmissible at trial.

If you are unsure whether to answer a question, ask your lawyer and follow his or her advice.

Your attorney also may object to inappropriate questions. If there is an objection, say nothing until the attorneys discuss the objection. You will be directed whether or not to answer.

5.16 What if I give incorrect information in my deposition?

You will be under oath during your deposition, so it is very important that you be truthful. If you give incorrect information by mistake, contact your attorney as soon as you realize the error. If you lie during your deposition, you risk being impeached by the other lawyer during your divorce trial. This could cause you to lose credibility with the court, rendering your testimony less valuable.

5.17 What if I don't know or can't remember the answer to a question?

You may be asked questions about which you have no knowledge. It is always acceptable to say "I don't know" if you do not have the knowledge. Similarly, if you cannot remember, simply say so.

5.18 What else do I need to know about having my deposition taken?

The following suggestions will help you give a successful deposition:

- Prepare for your deposition by reviewing and providing necessary documents and talking with your lawyer.

- Discuss with your lawyer in advance of your deposition whether you should review the transcript of your deposition for its accuracy or whether you should waive your right to review and sign the deposition.

- Get a good night's sleep the night before. Eat a meal with protein to sustain your energy, as the length of depositions can vary.

- Arrive early for your deposition so that you have time to get comfortable with your surroundings.

- Relax. You are going to be asked questions about matters that you know. Your deposition is likely to begin with routine matters such as your education and work history.

- Tell the truth, including whether you have met with an attorney or discussed preparation for the deposition.

- Stay calm. Your spouse's attorney will be judging your credibility and demeanor. Do not argue with the attorneys.

- Listen carefully to the entire question. Do not try to anticipate questions or start thinking about your answer before the attorney has finished asking the question.

- Take your time and carefully consider the question before answering. There is no need to hurry.

- If you do not understand the question clearly, ask that it be repeated or rephrased. Do not try to answer what you *think* was asked.

- Answer the question directly. If the question calls only for "yes" or "no," provide such an answer.

- Do not volunteer information. If the attorney wants to elicit more information, he or she will do so in following questions.

- If you do not know or cannot remember the answer, say so. This is an adequate answer.

- Do not guess. If your answer is an estimate or approximation, say so. Do not let an attorney pin you down to anything you are not sure about. For example, if you cannot remember the number of times an event occurred, say that. If the attorney asks you if it was more than ten times, answer only if you can. If you can provide a range (more than ten but less than twenty) with reasonable certainty, you may do so.

- If an attorney mischaracterizes something you said earlier, say so.

- Speak clearly and loudly enough for everyone to hear you.

- Answer all questions with words, rather than gestures or sounds. "Uh-huh" is difficult for the court reporter to distinguish from "uh-uh" and may result in inaccuracies in the transcript.

- If you need a break at any point in the deposition, you have the right to request one. You can talk to your attorney during such a break.

Remember, the purpose of your deposition is to support a good outcome in your case and completing it will help move your case forward.

5.19 Are depositions always necessary? Does every witness have to be deposed?

Depositions are less likely to be needed if you and your spouse are reaching agreement on most of the facts in your case and you are moving toward a settlement. They are more likely to be needed in cases where child custody is disputed or where there are complex financial issues. Although depositions of all witnesses are usually unnecessary, it is common to take depositions of expert witnesses.

5.20 Will I get a copy of the depositions in my case?

Ask your attorney for copies of the depositions in your case. It will be important for you to carefully review your deposition if your case proceeds to trial.

6

Mediation and Negotiation

If your marriage was full of conflict, you might be asking yourself how you can make the fighting stop. You picture your divorce as having vicious lawyers, an angry spouse, and screaming matches. You wonder if there is a way out of this nightmare.

Or, perhaps you and your spouse are parting ways amicably. Although you are in disagreement about how your divorce should be settled, you are clear that you want the process to be respectful and without hostility. You'd rather spend your hard-earned money on your children's college education than on legal fees.

In either case, going to trial and having a judge make all of the decisions in your divorce is not inevitable. In fact, most Tennessee divorce cases settle without the need for a trial.

Mediation and negotiation can help you and your spouse resolve your disputed issues and reach your own agreements without taking your case before the judge, who will make your decisions for you.

Resolving your divorce through a mediated or negotiated settlement has many advantages. You can achieve a mutually satisfying agreement, a known outcome, little risk of appeal, and often enjoy significantly lower legal fees. Despite the circumstances that led to the end of your marriage, it might be possible for your divorce to conclude peacefully with the help of these tools.

6.1   What is the difference between *mediation* and *negotiation*?

Both mediation and negotiation are methods used to help you and your spouse settle your divorce by reaching agreement rather than going to trial and having the judge make decisions for you. These methods are sometimes referred to as *alternative dispute resolution (ADR)*.

Mediation uses a trained mediator, often a lawyer experienced in divorce practice, who is an independent, neutral third party. He or she is a skilled professional who can assist you and your spouse in the process. *Negotiation* involves lawyers for both you and your spouse. Lawyers for the spouses may also be present during mediation, although their involvement is usually less than in negotiation.

6.2   How are mediation and negotiation different from a *collaborative* divorce?

Collaborative law is a method of resolving a divorce case where both parties have a strong commitment to settling their disputes and avoiding litigation. You and your spouse each hire an attorney trained in the collaborative law process. You and your lawyers enter into an agreement that provides that in the event either you or your spouse decides to take the case to court, both of you must terminate services with your collaborative lawyers and start anew.

Often, spouses in the collaborative process enlist the support of other professionals, such as an independent financial advisor or coaches, to support them through the process. Although the process may be lengthy, it enables the focus to shift away from the conflict and toward finding solutions. The attorneys become a part of the team supporting settlement rather than advocates adding to the conflict.

Talk to your lawyer about whether your case would be well suited to the collaborative law process.

6.3 What is involved in the mediation process? What will I have to do and how long will it take?

The mediation process will be explained to you in detail by the mediator at the start of the mediation session. Mediation involves one or more meetings with you, your spouse, and the mediator. In some cases the attorneys will also be present.

Prior to meeting with you and your spouse in an initial mediation session, the mediator will conduct an individual initial screening session with each of you to assess your ability to communicate with each other and to determine if there is indication of domestic abuse or other forms of intimidation or coercion. After the mediator's initial screening, he or she will decide whether you and your spouse should mediate together, or whether your mediation should take place separately.

The mediator will outline ground rules designed to ensure you will be treated respectfully and given an opportunity to be heard. In some cases, you and your spouse will each be given an opportunity to make opening remarks about what is important to you in the outcome of your divorce.

How long the process of mediation continues depends upon many of the same factors that affect how long your divorce will take. These include how many issues you and your spouse disagree about, the complexity of these issues, and the willingness of each of you to work toward an agreement.

Your case could settle after just one mediation session or it might require a series of meetings. It is common for the mediator to clarify at the close of each session whether the parties are willing to continue with another session.

6.4 My lawyer said that mediation and negotiation can reduce delays in completing my divorce. How can they do this?

When the issues in your divorce are decided by a judge instead of by you and your spouse, there are many opportunities for delay. These can include:

- Waiting for the trial date
- Having to return to court on a later, second date if your trial is not completed on the day it is scheduled
- Waiting for the judge's ruling on your case

- Needing additional court hearings after your trial to resolve disputes about the intention of your judge's rulings, issues that were overlooked, or disagreement regarding the language of the decree

Each one of these events holds the possibility of delaying your divorce by days, weeks, or even months. Mediating or negotiating the terms of your divorce decree can eliminate these delays.

6.5 How can mediation and negotiation lower the costs of my divorce?

If your case is not settled by agreement, you will be going to trial. If the issues in your case are many or if they are complex, such as custody, the attorney's fees and other costs of going to trial can be tremendous.

By settling your case without going to trial, you may be able to save thousands of dollars in legal fees. Ask your attorney for a litigation budget that sets forth the potential costs of going to trial, so that you have some idea of these costs when deciding whether to settle an issue or to take it to trial before the judge.

6.6 Are there other benefits to mediating or negotiating a settlement?

Yes. A divorce resolved by a mediated or negotiated agreement can have these additional benefits:

Recognizing Common Goals. Mediation and negotiation allow for brainstorming between the parties and attorneys. Looking at all possible solutions, even impractical ones, invites creative solutions to common goals. For example, suppose you and your spouse both agree you need to pay your spouse some amount of equity for the family home you will keep, but you have no cash to make the payment. Together, you may come up with a number of options for accomplishing your goal and select the best one. Contrast this with a judge simply ordering you to pay the money without considering all of the possible options.

Addressing the Unique Circumstances of Your Situation.
Rather than using a one-size-fits-all approach as a judge might,
a settlement reached by agreement allows you and your
spouse to consider the unique circumstances of your situation
in formulating a good outcome. For example, suppose you
disagree about parenting times for the Thanksgiving holiday.
The judge might order you to alternate the holiday each year,
although you both would have preferred to have your child
share the day.

Creating a Safe Place for Communication. Mediation and
negotiation give each party an opportunity to be heard. Perhaps you and your spouse have not yet had an opportunity to
directly share your concerns about settlement with one another. For example, you may be worried about how the temporary
parenting time arrangement is affecting your children, but have
not yet discussed it with your spouse. A mediation session or
settlement conference can be a safe place for the two of you to
communicate concerns about your children or your finances.

Fulfilling Your Children's Needs. You may see that your
children would be better served by you and your spouse
deciding their future rather than having it decided by a judge
who does not know, love, and understand your children like
the two of you do.

Eliminating the Risk and Uncertainty of Trial. If a judge
decides the outcome of your divorce, you give up control
over the terms of the settlement. The decisions are left in the
hands of the judge. If you and your spouse reach agreement,
however, you have the power to eliminate the risk of an
uncertain outcome.

Reducing the Risk of Harm to Your Children. If your case
goes to trial, it is likely you and your spouse will give testimony
that will be upsetting to each other. As the conflict increases,
the relationship between you and your spouse inevitably
deteriorates. This can be harmful to your children. Contrast this
with mediation or settlement negotiations, in which you open
your communication and seek to reach agreement. It is not
unusual for the relationship between the parents to improve
as the professionals create a safe environment for rebuilding

communication and reaching agreements in the best interests of a child.

Having the Support of Professionals. Using trained professionals, such as mediators and attorneys, to support you can help you to reach a settlement you may think is impossible. These professionals have skills to help you focus on what is most important to you, and shift your attention away from irrelevant facts. They understand the law and know the possible outcomes if your case goes to trial.

Lowering Stress. The process of preparing for and going to court can be stressful. Your energy is also going toward caring for your children, looking at your finances, and coping with the emotions of divorce. You might decide you would be better served by settling your case rather than proceeding to trial.

Achieving Closure. When you are going through a divorce, the process can feel as though it is taking an eternity. By reaching agreement, you and your spouse are better able to put the divorce behind you and move forward with your lives.

6.7 Is mediation mandatory?

Although mediation is not mandatory prior to filing for divorce in Tennessee, mediation is mandatory after a divorce filing if you are unable to settle the case between yourselves or your lawyers.

6.8 My spouse was mentally and physically abusive to me. Should I participate in mediation anyway?

If you have been a victim of domestic violence by your spouse, it is important that you discuss the appropriateness of mediation with your attorney. Mediation may not be a safe way for you to reach agreement and the judge may waive the mediation requirement.

Prior to allowing mediation to proceed, any mediator should ask you whether you have been a victim of domestic violence. This is critical for the mediator to both assess your safety and to ensure that the balance of power in the mediation process is maintained.

Talk with your attorney if you have experienced domestic violence or if you feel threatened or intimidated by your spouse. It may be possible to mediate with you and your spouse in different rooms or during separate sessions.

If you feel threatened or intimidated by your spouse but still want to proceed with mediation, talk to your attorney about him or her attending the mediation sessions with you. Request to have the mediation occur at your lawyer's office, where you feel more comfortable. If you do participate in mediation, insist that your mediator have a good understanding of the dynamics of domestic abuse and how they can impact the mediation process.

6.9   How is the mediator selected?

Most mediators in Tennessee are attorneys who have extensive experience in divorce law and litigation in Tennessee. Often, the attorneys in a case are able to agree upon a mediator. If the attorneys are unable to agree upon a mediator, the judge will appoint a *Rule 31 mediator.* This type of mediator has been through a thirty-hour mediation class and certified by the state of Tennessee.

6.10   What types of issues can be mediated or negotiated?

All of the issues in your case can be mediated or negotiated. However, in advance of any mediation or negotiation session, you should discuss with your lawyer which issues you want to be mediated or negotiated.

Tennessee law requires that you participate in mediation of matters concerning your children. Talk with your lawyer in advance of any mediation about custody to be absolutely clear about the impact of custody decisions on child support. Agreeing to certain custody terms can drastically reduce child support, and you should not negotiate on child custody and parenting time without having first fully discussed with your attorney its impact on child support.

You may decide that certain issues are nonnegotiable for you. Discuss this with your attorney in advance of any mediation or negotiation sessions so that he or she can support you in focusing the discussions on the issues you are open to looking at.

6.11 What is the role of my attorney in the mediation process?

The role of your attorney in the mediation process will vary depending upon your situation. Your attorney can assist you in identifying which issues will be discussed in mediation and which are better left to negotiation between the lawyers or to the judge.

If you have minor children, it is essential that you discuss with your attorney how sharing physical custody of your children can significantly lower child support. In all cases it is important that your attorney review any agreements discussed in mediation before a final agreement is reached.

6.12 How do I prepare for mediation?

Prior to attending a mediation session with your spouse, discuss with your attorney the issues you intend to mediate. In particular, be sure to discuss the impact of custody and parenting time arrangements on child support.

Enlist your attorney's support in identifying your intentions for the mediation. Make a list of the issues important to you. For example, when it comes to your child, you might consider whether it is your child's safety, the parenting time schedule, or the ability to attend your children's events which concerns you most.

Be forward looking. Giving thought to your desired outcomes while approaching mediation with an open mind and heart is the best way to move closer to settlement.

6.13 Do children attend the mediation sessions?

In most cases your child will not participate in the mediation. However, your case might be an exception if you have an older child who is sufficiently mature to participate in the process.

If you think your child should be at the mediation table, talk to your lawyer and your mediator about the potential risks and benefits of including him or her in the process.

6.14 I want my attorney to look over the agreements my spouse and I discussed in mediation before I give my final approval. Is this possible?

Absolutely. Before giving your written or final approval to any agreements reached in mediation, it is critical that your attorney review the agreements first. This is necessary to ensure that you understand the terms of the settlement and its implications. Your attorney will also review the agreement for compliance with Tennessee law.

6.15 Who pays for mediation?

The cost of mediation must be paid for by you or your spouse. Often, it is a shared expense. Expect your mediator to address the matter of fees before or at your first session.

6.16 What if mediation fails?

If mediation is not successful, you still may be able to settle your case through negotiations between the attorneys. Also, you and your spouse can agree to preserve the settlements that were reached and to take only the remaining disputed issues to the judge for trial.

6.17 What is a *settlement conference*?

A *settlement conference* can be a powerful tool for the resolution of your case. It is a meeting held with you, your spouse, and your lawyers with the intention of negotiating the terms of your divorce. In some cases, a professional with important information needed to support the settlement process, such as an accountant, also may participate.

Settlement conferences are most effective when both parties and their attorneys see the potential for a negotiated resolution and have the necessary information to accomplish that goal.

6.18 Why should I consider a settlement conference when the attorneys can negotiate through letters and phone calls?

A settlement conference can eliminate the delays that often occur when negotiation takes place through correspondence and calls between the attorneys. Rather than waiting days or weeks for a response, you can receive a response on a proposal in a matter of minutes.

A settlement conference also enables you and your spouse, if you choose, to use your own words to explain the reasoning behind your requests. You are also able to provide information immediately to expedite the process.

6.19 How do I prepare for my settlement conference?

Being well prepared for the settlement conference can help you make the most of this opportunity to resolve your case without the need for trial. Actions you should take include:

- Provide in advance of the conference all necessary information. If your attorney has asked you for a current pay stub, tax return, debt amounts, asset values, or other documentation, make sure you provide it prior to the meeting.

- Discuss your topics of concern with your attorney in advance. Your attorney can assist you in understanding your rights under the law so you can have realistic expectations for the outcome of negotiations.

- Bring a positive attitude, a listening ear, and an open mind. Come with the attitude that your case will settle. Be willing to listen to the opposing party. Resist the urge to interrupt.

Few cases settle without each side demonstrating flexibility and a willingness to compromise. Most cases settle when parties are able to bring these positive qualities to the process.

6.20 What will happen at my settlement conference?

Typically, the conference will be held at the office of one of the attorneys, with both parties and lawyers present. If there are a number of issues to be discussed, an agenda may be used to keep the focus on relevant topics. From time to time throughout the conference, you and your attorney may meet alone to consult as needed. If additional information is needed to reach agreement, some issues may be set aside for later discussion.

The length of the conference depends upon the number of issues to be resolved, the complexity of the issues, and the willingness of the parties and lawyers to communicate effectively. An effort is made to confirm which issues are resolved and which issues remain disputed. Then, one by one, the issues are addressed.

6.21 What is the role of my attorney in the settlement conference?

Your attorney is your advocate during the settlement conference. You can count on him or her to support you throughout the process, to see that important issues are addressed, and to counsel you privately outside of the presence of your spouse and his or her lawyer.

6.22 Why is my attorney appearing so friendly with my spouse and her attorney?

Successful negotiations rely upon building trust between the parties working toward agreement. Your lawyer may be respectful or pleasant toward your spouse or your spouse's lawyer to promote a good outcome for you.

6.23 What happens if my spouse and I settled some but not all of the issues in our divorce?

You and your spouse can agree to maintain the agreements you have reached and let the judge decide those matters that you are unable to resolve. Talk to your lawyer about the advantages and disadvantages of settling parts, but not all, of your case.

6.24 If my spouse and I reach an agreement, how long will it take before it can be finalized?

If a settlement is reached through negotiation or mediation, one of the attorneys will put the agreement in writing for approval by you and your spouse. If you or your spouse request a final hearing and the sixty-or ninety-day waiting period has expired, in most cases, a final hearing is held within thirty days of the agreement being signed. If there is not a final hearing, your agreement is submitted to the judge for approval and is usually finalized in several business days.

7

Emergency:
When You Fear Your Spouse

Suddenly you are in a panic. Maybe your spouse was serious when threatening to take your child and leave the state. What if you are kicked out of your own home? Suppose all of the bank accounts are emptied. Your fear heightens as your mind spins with every horror story you have heard about divorce.

Facing an emergency situation in divorce can feel as though your entire life is at stake. You may not be able to concentrate on anything else. At the same time, you may be paralyzed with anxiety and have no idea how to begin to protect yourself. No doubt you have countless worries about what your future holds.

When facing an emergency, do your best to focus on what to do in the immediate moment. Set aside your worries about the future for another day. Let others support you, and start taking action right away.

Remember, you have overcome many challenges in your life before this moment. There are people willing to help you. Step by step, you will make it through again this time.

7.1   My spouse has deserted me, and I need to get divorced as quickly as possible. What is my first step?

Your first step is to seek legal advice at your earliest opportunity. The earlier you get legal counsel to advise you about your rights, the better. The initial consultation with an attorney will answer most of your questions and start you on an action plan for getting your divorce underway.

7.2 I'm afraid my abusive spouse will try to hurt me and/ or our children if I say I want a divorce. What can I do legally to protect myself and my children?

Develop a plan with your safety and that of your children as your highest priority. In addition to meeting with an attorney at your first opportunity, develop a safety plan in the event you and your children need to escape your home. A great way to do this is to let in support from an agency that helps victims of domestic violence.

Your risk of harm from an abusive spouse increases when you leave. For this reason, all actions must be taken with safety as the first concern. Call the clerk's office at your local justice center or courthouse to determine the base place to seek information regarding domestic violence.

Find a lawyer who understands domestic violence. Often, your local domestic violence agency can help with a referral. Talk to your lawyer about the concerns for your safety and that of your children. Ask your lawyer about an *order of protection.* This is a court order that may offer a number of protections including granting you temporary custody of your children for up to one year and ordering your spouse to leave the family residence and have no contact with you.

7.3 I am afraid to meet with an attorney because I am terrified my spouse will find out and get violent. What should I do?

Schedule an initial consultation with an attorney who is experienced in working with domestic violence victims. When you schedule the appointment, let the firm know your situation and instruct the law office not to place any calls to you that you think your spouse might discover. If possible, pay for your consultation in cash.

Consultations with your attorney are confidential. Your attorney has an ethical duty to not disclose your meeting with anyone outside the law firm. Let your attorney know your concerns so extra precautions can be taken by the law office in handling your file.

7.4 I want to give my attorney all the information needed so my children and I are safe from my spouse. What does this include?

Provide your attorney with complete information about the history, background, nature, and evidence of your abuse including:

- Types of abuse (for example, physical, sexual, verbal, financial, mental, emotional)
- Dates, time frames, or occasions
- The locations
- Whether you were ever medically treated
- Any police reports made
- E-mails, letters, notes, or journal entries indicating the abuse
- Photographs taken
- Witnesses to the abuse or evidence of the abuse
- Statements made by your spouse admitting the abuse
- Alcohol or drug abuse by your spouse
- The possession or use of guns or other weapons by your spouse

The better the information you provide to your attorney, the easier it will be for him or her to make a strong case for the protection of you and your children.

7.5 I'm not ready to hire an lawyer for a divorce, but I am afraid my spouse is going to get violent with my children and me in the meantime. What can I do?

It is possible to seek an order of protection from the court without an attorney. It is possible for the judge to order your spouse out of your home, granting you custody of your children for up to one year, and order your spouse to stay away from you.

7.6 What is the difference between a *domestic abuse protection order* and a *restraining order*?

Orders of protection and restraining orders are court orders directing a person to not engage in certain behavior. Each of them are intended to protect people from abusers. Although any of the orders can initially be obtained without notice to the other spouse, that spouse always has a right to a hearing to determine whether an order of protection or restraining order should remain in place.

Talk to your attorney about obtaining an *order of protection* if you are concerned about your safety, your children's safety, or if there has been a history of domestic abuse. If your spouse has attempted to cause, has caused or has threatened to cause you bodily injury, you may qualify for a *domestic abuse protection order*. The violation of a domestic abuse protection order is a criminal offense, which can result in immediate arrest.

If you are concerned that your spouse will annoy, threaten, harass, or intimidate you after your divorce complaint is filed, ask your lawyer about a restraining order. A *restraining order* is a court order that prohibits a person from engaging in behavior that has been restrained by the court. If your spouse violates the restraining order, he or she may be brought before the court for contempt.

7.7 My spouse has been harassing me since I filed for divorce. What can I do?

It may be possible to seek a harassment protection order from the court. In order to qualify for a harassment protection order, you must be able to prove that your spouse has engaged in a knowing and willful course of conduct that seriously terrifies, threatens, or intimidates you. Talk with your lawyer about whether you should seek the court's protection from your spouse.

7.8   My spouse has never been violent, but I know she is going to be really angry and upset when the divorce papers are served. Do I need a protection order?

The facts of your case may not warrant an order of protection. In all Tennessee divorce cases, a standard restraining order is issued. It states that:

NOTICE TO BOTH PARTIES OF INJUNCTIONS IN DIVORCE

Pursuant to Tenn. Code Ann. § 36-4-106(d), the following temporary injunctions are in effect upon both parties upon the filing of a petition for divorce or legal separation, except on the sole grounds of irreconcilable difference, and upon personal service of the complaint and summons on the respondent or upon waiver and acceptance of service by the respondent with these provisions attached to the complaint and summons.

These temporary injunctions are in effect until the:

1. final decree of divorce or order of legal separation is entered,

2. petition is dismissed,

3. parties reach agreement, or

4. Court modifies or dissolves the injunction.

Both parties are restrained and enjoined from:

1. Transferring, assigning, borrowing against, concealing or in any way dissipating or disposing of, without the consent of the other party or an order of the court, any marital property; (Expenditures from current income to maintain the marital standard of living and the usual and ordinary costs of operating a business are not restricted by this injunction. Each party shall maintain records of all expenditures, copies of which shall be available to the other party upon request.)

2. Voluntarily concealing, modifying, terminating, assigning or allowing to lapse for non-

payment of premiums, any insurance policy, including but not limited to life, health, disability, homeowners, renters and automobile, where such insurance policy provides coverage to either of the parties or that names either of the parties as beneficiaries, without the consent of the other party or an order of the court;

3. Harassing, threatening, assaulting or abusing the other and from making disparaging remarks about the other to or in the presence of any children of the parties or to either party's employer, and;

4. Relocating any children of the parties outside the State of Tennessee, or more than 100 miles from the marital home, without the permission of the other party or an order of the Court, except in the case of a removal based upon a well-founded fear of physical abuse against either the fleeing parent or the child. In such case, upon request of the non-relocating parent, the Court will conduct an expedited hearing, by phone conference if appropriate, to determine the reasonableness of the relocation and to make such other orders as appropriate.

This does not in any way preclude either of the parties from seeking broader injunctive relief from the court.

7.9 I'm afraid my spouse is going to take all of the money out of our bank accounts and leave me with nothing. What can I do?

Talk to your attorney immediately. If you are worried about your spouse emptying financial accounts or selling marital assets, it is critical that you take action at once. Your attorney can advise you on your right to take possession of certain assets in order to protect them from being hidden or spent by your spouse. Also, you have some protection from the automatic restraining order referenced in question 7.8.

7.10 My spouse says I am crazy, a liar, and that no judge will ever believe me if I tell the truth about the abusive behavior. What can I do if I don't have any proof?

Most domestic violence is not witnessed by third parties. Often, there is little physical evidence. Even without physical evidence, a judge can enter orders to protect you and your children if you give truthful testimony about your abuse which the judge finds believable. Your own testimony of your abuse is evidence.

It is very common for persons who abuse others to claim that their victims are liars and to make statements intended to discourage disclosure of the abuse. This is yet another form of controlling behavior.

Your attorney's skills and experience will support you to give effective testimony in the courtroom to establish your case. Let your lawyer know your concerns so that a strong case can be presented to the judge based upon your persuasive statements of the truth of your experience.

7.11 My spouse told me that if I ever file for divorce, I'll never see my child again. Should I be worried about my child being abducted?

Your fear that your spouse will abduct your child is a common one. It is quite rare for a parent to actually abduct a child. It can be helpful to look at some of the factors that appear to increase the risk that your child will be abducted by the other parent. Most abductions are made by men. They are often from marriages that cross culture, race, religion, or ethnicity. A lower socioeconomic status, prior criminal record, and limited social or economic ties to the community can also increase risk.

Programming and brainwashing are almost always present in cases where a child is at risk for being kidnapped by a parent, and efforts to isolate the child may also be seen. Exit activities such as obtaining a new passport, getting financial matters in order, or contacting a moving company could be indicators.

Talk to your lawyer to assess the risks in your particular case. Together you can determine whether statements by your spouse are threats intended to control or intimidate you or whether legal action is needed to protect your child.

7.12 What legal steps can be taken to prevent my spouse from removing our child from the state?

In Tennessee, upon the filing of a divorce, a restraining order from relocating with a child out of state is automatically entered. If you are concerned about your child being removed from the state, ask your lawyer whether any of these options might be available in your case:

- A court order giving you immediate custody until a temporary custody hearing can be held
- A court order directing your spouse to turn over passports for the child and your spouse to the court
- The posting of a bond prior to your spouse exercising parenting time
- Supervised visitation

Both state and federal laws are designed to provide protection from the unlawful removal of children from one state to another when a custody matter is brought and to protect children from kidnapping. *The Uniform Child Custody Jurisdiction Enforcement Act (UCCJEA)* was passed to encourage the custody of children to be decided in the state where they have been living most recently and where they have the most ties. *The Parental Kidnapping Prevention Act (PKPA)* makes it a federal crime for a parent to kidnap a child in violation of a valid custody order.

If you are concerned about your child being abducted, talk with your lawyer about all options available to you for your child's protection.

7.13 How quickly can I get a divorce in Tennessee?

There are a number of time requirements for getting a divorce in Tennessee. Either you or your spouse must have been a resident of Tennessee for more than six months immediately prior to the filing of the complaint for the divorce with the court. After you file your divorce, your spouse must be given notice of the divorce.

A sixty-day or ninety-day waiting period, depending on whether children are involved, is required for every Tennessee divorce. This period begins on the date the divorce complaint is filed with the court.

The soonest your case can be resolved is after the sixty-day or ninety-day waiting period has expired, although most cases do not resolve this quickly. The length of time your case remains pending depends in large part upon the extent to which you and your spouse reach agreement on the issues in your case.

Your divorce becomes final for most purposes thirty days after the judge signs your divorce decree.

7.14   If either my spouse or I file for divorce, will I be ordered out of my home? Who decides who gets to live in the house while we go through the divorce?

If you and your spouse cannot reach an agreement regarding which of you will leave the residence during the divorce, the judge will decide whether one of you should be granted exclusive possession of the home until the case is concluded. In some cases judges have been known to refuse to order either party out of the house until the divorce is concluded.

Abusive behavior is one basis for seeking temporary possession of the home. If there are minor children, the custodial parent will ordinarily be awarded temporary possession of the residence.

Other factors the judge may consider include:

- Whether one of you owned the home prior to the marriage
- After provisions are made for payment of temporary support, who can afford to remain in the home or obtain other housing
- Who is most likely to be awarded the home in the divorce
- Options available to each of you for other temporary housing, including other homes or family members who live in the area

- Special needs that would make a move unduly burdensome, such as a health condition
- Self-employment from home, which could not be readily moved, such as a child-care business

If staying in the home is important to you, talk to your attorney about your reasons so that a strong case can be made for you at the temporary hearing.

8

Child Custody

Ever since you and your spouse began talking about divorce, chances are your children have been your greatest concern. You or your spouse might have postponed the decision to seek divorce because of concern about the impact on your children. Now that the time has come, you might still have doubts about whether your children will be all right after the divorce.

Remember that you have been making wise and loving decisions for your children since they were born. You've always done your best to see that they had everything they really needed. You loved them and protected them. This won't change because you are going through your divorce. You were a good parent before the divorce and you will be a good parent after the divorce.

It can be difficult not to worry about how the sharing of parenting time with your spouse will affect your children. You may also have fears about being cut out of your child's life. Try to remember that, regardless of who has custody, it is likely that the court order will not only give you a lot of time with your children but also a generous opportunity to be involved in their day-to-day lives.

With the help of your lawyer, you can make sound decisions regarding the custody arrangement that is in the best interests of your children.

8.1   What is *custody* in Tennessee?

For practical purposes, we use the term *custody* thoughout this book. But in Tennessee, courts do not typically use the term custody. In Tennessee, a *primary residential parent* (the parent who has custody) is named and an *alternate residential parent* (noncustodial parent) is named. In some cases, the parties agree to an equal share of the parenting time (joint custody).

In Tennessee, each spouse signs a proposed *parenting plan* at the outset of the divorce. This is a document signed under oath that proposes your plan for how the parents should share parenting time, in the best interests of your child or children. If the parties can agree on a permanent parenting plan, it will typically be approved by the court. If the parties cannot agree, a judge will order a permanent parenting plan.

Sample Parenting Plan

PERMANENT PARENTING PLAN ORDER

STATE OF TENNESSEE

COURT_____   COUNTY_____

FILE No._____   DIVISION_____

☐ PROPOSED ☐ AGREED ☐ ORDERED BY THE COURT

PLAINTIFF:_____ ☐ Mother ☐ Father

DEFENDANT:_____ ☐ Mother ☐ Father

The mother and father will behave with each other and each child so as to provide a loving, stable, consistent and nurturing relationship with the child even though they are divorced. They will not speak badly of each other or the members of the family of the other parent. They will encourage each child to continue to love the other parent and be comfortable in both families.

This plan   ☐ is a new plan.

　　　　　☐ modifies an existing Parenting Plan dated_____

　　　　　☐ modifies an existing Order dated_____

Child's Name   Date of Birth

_____   _____

_____   _____

_____   _____

_____   _____

I. RESIDENTIAL PARENTING SCHEDULE

A.   RESIDENTIAL TIME WITH EACH PARENT

The Primary Residential Parent is_____

Under the schedule set forth below, each parent will spend the following number of days with the children:

Mother_____days   Father_____days

B.   DAY -TO-DAY SCHEDULE

The mother father shall have responsibility for the care of the child or children except at the following times when the other parent shall have responsibility:

From_____to_____

    Day and Time   Day and Time

☐ every week   ☐ every other week   ☐ other:

The other parent shall also have responsibility for the care of the child or children at the additional parenting times specified below:

From_____to_____

    Day and Time   Day and Time

☐ every week   ☐ every other week   ☐ other:

This parenting schedule begins ☐_____

or.☐ date of the Court's Order.   Day and Time

C.   HOLIDAY SCHEDULE AND OTHER SCHOOL FREE DAYS

Indicate if child or children will be with parent in ODD or EVEN numbered years or EVERY year:

	MOTHER	FATHER
New Year's Day	_____	_____
Martin Luther King Day	_____	_____
Presidents' Day	_____	_____
Easter Day	_____	_____
Passover Day	_____	_____

Child Custody

Mother's Day	_____	_____
Memorial Day	_____	_____
Father's Day	_____	_____
July 4th	_____	_____
Labor Day	_____	_____
Halloween	_____	_____
Thanksgiving Day & Friday	_____	_____
Children's Birthdays	_____	_____
Other School-Free Days	_____	_____
Mother's Birthday	_____	_____
Father's Birthday	_____	_____
Other:	_____	_____

A holiday shall begin at 6:00 p.m. on the night preceding the holiday and end at 6:00 p.m. the night of the holiday, unless otherwise noted here

D. FALL VACATION (If applicable)

The day to day schedule shall apply except as follows:_____
beginning_____.

E. WINTER (CHRISTMAS) VACATION

The ☐ mother ☐ father shall have the child or children for the first period from the day and time school is dismissed until December_____at_____a.m/p.m. ☐ in odd-numbered years ☐ in even-numbered years ☐ every year. The other parent will have the child or children for the second period from the day and time indicated above until 6:00 p.m. on the evening before school resumes. The parties shall alternate the first and second periods each year.

Other agreement of the parents:

_____

F. SPRING VACATION (If applicable)

The day-to-day schedule shall apply except as follows:
_____beginning_____.

G. SUMMER VACATION

The day-to-day schedule shall apply except as follows: _____beginning_____.
Is written notice required? ☐ Yes ☐ No. If so, number of days.

H. TRANSPORTATION ARRANGEMENTS

The place of meeting for the exchange of the child or children shall be:_____.
Payment of long-distance transportation costs (if applicable): ☐ mother ☐ father ☐ both equally.
Other arrangements:_____.
If a parent does not possess a valid driver's license, he or she must make reasonable transportation arrangements to protect the child or children while in the care of that parent.

I. SUPERVISION OF PARENTING TIME (If applicable)

☐ Check if applicable
Supervised parenting time shall apply during the day-to-day schedule as follows:
☐ Place:

_____

☐ Person or organization supervising:

_____

☐ Responsibility for cost, if any: ☐ mother ☐ father ☐ both equally.

J. OTHER

The following special provisions apply:

_____
_____

II. DECISION MAKING

A. DAY-TO-DAY DECISIONS

Each parent shall make decisions regarding the day-to-day care of a child while the child is residing with that parent, including any emergency decisions affecting the health or safety of a child.

B. MAJOR DECISIONS

Major decisions regarding each child shall be made as follows:

Educational decisions ☐ mother ☐ father ☐ joint
Nonemergency health care ☐ mother ☐ father ☐ joint
Religious upbringing ☐ mother ☐ father ☐ joint
Extracurricular activities ☐ mother ☐ father ☐ joint
_____ ☐ mother ☐ father ☐ joint

III. FINANCIAL SUPPORT

A. CHILD SUPPORT

Father's gross monthly income is $_____
Mother's gross monthly income is $_____

1. The final child-support order is as follows:

   a. The ☐ mother ☐ father shall pay to the other parent as regular child support the sum of ☐ weekly ☐ monthly ☐ twice per month

☐ every two weeks. The Child Support Worksheet shall be attached to this Order as an Exhibit.*

If this is a deviation from the Child Support Guidelines, explain why:_____
_____.

2. Retroactive Support: A judgment is hereby awarded in the amount of $_____ to ☐ mother ☐ father against the child-support payor representing retroactive support required under Section 1240-2-4.06 of the D.H.S. Income Shares Child Support Guidelines dating from which shall be paid (including pre/post judgment interest) at the rate of $_____per ☐ week ☐ month ☐ twice per month ☐ every two weeks until the judgment is paid in full.

3. Payments shall begin on the____day of_____, 20_.
This support shall be paid:

☐ directly to the other parent.

☐ to the Central Child Support Receipting Unit, P. O. Box 305200, Nashville,Tennessee 37229, and sent from there to the other parent at:

☐ A Wage Assignment Order is attached to this Parenting Plan.

☐ by direct deposit to the other parent at bank for deposit in account no._____.

☐ income assignment not required; Explanation:_____.

☐ other:_____.

The parents acknowledge that court approval must be obtained before child support can be reduced or modified.

*Child Support Worksheet can be found on DHS website at www.state. tn.us/humanserv/is/isdocuments.html or at your local child support offices.

B.   FEDERAL INCOME TAX EXEMPTION[1]

The ☐ mother ☐ father is the parent receiving child support. The mother shall claim the following children:

_____

_____

The father shall claim the following children:

_____

_____

[1]NOTE: The child-support schedule assumptions in the guidelines (1240-2-4-.03 (6)(b)) assume that the parent receiving the child support will get the tax exemptions for the child.

The ☐ mother ☐ father may claim the exemptions for the child or children so long as child support payments are current by the claiming parent on January 15 of the year when the return is due. The exemptions may be claimed in: ☐ alternate years starting _____☐ each year ☐ other:_____

The ☐ mother ☐ father will furnish IRS Form 8332 to the parent entitled to the exemption by February 15 of the year the tax return is due.

C.   PROOF OF INCOME AND WORK-RELATED CHILD-CARE EXPENSES

Each parent shall send proof of income to the other parent for the prior calendar year as follows:

- IRS Forms W-2 and 1099 shall be sent to the other parent on or before February 15.
- A copy of his or her federal income tax return shall be sent to the other parent on or before April 15 or any later date when it is due because of an extension of time for filing.
- The completed form required by the Department of Human Services shall be sent to the Department on or before the date the federal income tax return is due by the parent paying child support. This requirement applies only if a parent is receiving benefits from the Department for a child.

The parent paying work-related child-care expenses shall send proof of expenses to the other parent for the prior calendar year and an estimate for the next calendar year, on or before February 15.

D. HEALTH AND DENTAL INSURANCE

Reasonable health insurance on the child or children will be:

☐ maintained by the mother
☐ maintained by the father
☐ maintained by both

Proof of continuing coverage shall be furnished to the other parent annually or as coverage changes. The parent maintaining coverage shall authorize the other parent to consult with the insurance carrier regarding the coverage in effect.

Uncovered reasonable and necessary medical expenses, which may include but is not limited to, deductibles or co-payments, eyeglasses, contact lens, routine annual physicals, and counseling will be paid by ☐ mother ☐ father ☐ *pro rata* in accordance with their incomes. After insurance has paid its portion, the parent receiving the bill will send it to the other parent within ten days. The other parent will pay his or her share within 30 days of receipt of the bill.

If available through work, the ☐ mother ☐ father shall maintain dental, orthodontic, and optical insurance on the minor child or children.

E. LIFE INSURANCE

If agreed upon by the parties, the ☐ mother ☐ father ☐ both shall insure his/her own life in the minimum amount of $_____by whole life or term insurance. Until the child-support obligation has been completed, each policy shall name the child/children as sole irrevocable primary beneficiary, with the ☐ other parent ☐ other_____, as trustee for the benefit of the child(ren), to serve without bond or accounting.

IV. PRIMARY RESIDENTIAL PARENT (CUSTODIAN) FOR OTHER LEGAL PURPOSES

The child or children are scheduled to reside the majority of the time with the ☐ mother ☐ father. This parent is designated as the primary residential parent also known as the custodian, SOLELY for purposes of any other applicable state and federal laws. If the parents are listed in Section II as joint decision makers, then, for purposes of obtaining health or other insurance, they shall be considered to be joint custodians. THIS DESIGNATION DOES NOT AFFECT EITHER PARENT'S RIGHTS OR RESPONSIBILITIES UNDER THIS PARENTING PLAN.

V. DISAGREEMENTS OR MODIFICATION OF PLAN

Should the parents disagree about this Parenting Plan or wish to modify it, they must make a good-faith effort to resolve the issue by the process selected below before returning to Court. Except for financial support issues including child support, health and dental insurance, uncovered medical and dental expenses, and life insurance, disputes must be submitted to:

☐ Mediation by a neutral party chosen by the parents or the Court.

☐ Arbitration by a neutral party selected by parents or the Court.

☐ The Court DUE TO ORDER OF PROTECTION OR RESTRICTIONS.

The costs of this process may be determined by the alternative dispute process or may be assessed by the Court

Child Custody

based upon the incomes of the parents. It must be commenced by notifying the other parent and the Court by ☐ written request ☐ certified mail ☐ other:_____.

In the dispute resolution process:

A. Preference shall be given to carrying out this Parenting Plan.

B. The parents shall use the process to resolve disputes relating to implementation of the Plan.

C. A written record shall be prepared of any agreement reached, and it shall be provided to each parent.

D. If the Court finds that a parent willfully failed to appear without good reason, the Court, upon motion, may award attorney fees and financial sanctions to the prevailing parent.

VI.   RIGHTS OF PARENTS

Under T.C.A. § 36-6-101 of Tennessee law, both parents are entitled to the following rights:

1. The right to unimpeded telephone conversations with the child at least twice a week at reasonable times and for reasonable durations;

2. The right to send mail to the child which the other parent shall not open or censor;

3. The right to receive notice and relevant information as soon as practicable but within twenty-four (24) hours of any event of hospitalization, major illness or death of the child;

4. The right to receive directly from the child's school any school records customarily made available to parents. (The school may require a written request which includes a current mailing address and upon payment of reasonable costs of duplicating.) These include copies of the child's report cards, attendance records, names of teachers, class schedules, and standardized test scores;

5. Unless otherwise provided by law, the right to receive copies of the child's medical health or other treatment records directly from the physician or health care

provider who provided treatment or health care. (The keeper of the records may require a written request which contains a current mailing address and the payment of reasonable costs of duplication.) No person who receives the mailing address of a parent as a result of this requirement shall provide such address to the other parent or a third person;

6. The right to be free of unwarranted derogatory remarks made about the parent or his or her family by the other parent to the child or in the presence of the child;

7. The right to be given at least forty-eight (48) hours' notice, whenever possible, of all extracurricular activities, and the opportunity to participate or observe them. These include the following: school activities, athletic activities, church activities and other activities where parental participation or observation would be appropriate;

8. The right to receive from the other parent, in the event the other parent leaves the state with the minor child or children for more than two (2) days, an itinerary including telephone numbers for use in the event of an emergency;

9. The right to access and participation in education on the same basis that is provided to all parents. This includes the right of access to the child for lunch and other activities. However participation or access must be reasonable and not interfere with day-to-day operations or with the child's educational performance.

VII.   NOTICE REGARDING PARENTAL RELOCATION

The Tennessee statute (T.C.A. § 36-6-108), which governs the notice to be given in connection with the relocation of a parent reads in pertinent part as follows:

If a parent who is spending intervals of time with a child desires to relocate outside the state or more than fifty (50) miles from the other parent within the state, the relocating parent shall send a notice to the other parent at the other parent's last known address by registered or certified mail. Unless excused by the court for exigent circumstances, the notice shall be mailed not later than sixty (60) days prior to the move. The notice shall contain the following:

1. Statement of intent to move;
2. Location of proposed new residence;
3. Reasons for proposed relocation; and
4. Statement that the other parent may file a petition in opposition to the move within thirty (30) days of receipt of the notice.

VIII.   PARENT EDUCATION CLASS

This requirement has been fulfilled by ☐ both parents ☐ mother ☐ father ☐ neither. Failure to attend the parent education class within 60 days of this order is punishable by contempt.

Under penalty of perjury, we declare that this plan has been proposed in good faith and is in the best interest of each minor child and that the statements herein and on the attached child-support worksheets are true and correct. (A notary public is required if this is a proposed plan by one parent rather than one agreed by both parents.)

_____   _____
Mother   Date and Place Signed

Sworn to and subscribed before me this_____day of __20_.
My commission expires:_____   _____
                                                        Notary Public

_____   _____
Father   Date and Place Signed

Sworn to and subscribed before me this_____day of __20_.
My commission expires:_____   _____
                                                        Notary Public

APPROVED FOR ENTRY:

Attorney for Mother

Address

Address

Phone and BPR Number

Attorney for Father

Address

Address

Phone and BPR Number

Note: The judge or chancellor may sign below or, instead, sign a Final Decree or a separate Order incorporating this plan.

COURT COSTS (If applicable)
Court costs, if any, are taxed as follows:

_____.

It is so ORDERED this the___day of_____,20__.

Judge or Chancellor

8.2   On what basis will the judge award custody?

The judge considers many factors in determining child custody. Most important is "the best interests of the child." To determine best interests, the judge may look at the following factors:

Home Environments. This refers to the respective environments offered by you and your spouse. The court may consider factors such as the safety, stability, and nurturing found in each home.

Emotional Ties. The emotional relationship between the child and each parent may include the nature of the bond between the parent and child and the feelings shared between the child and each parent.

Child Custody

Age, Sex, and Health of the Child and Parents. Tennessee no longer ascribes to the "tender years" doctrine, which formerly gave a preference for custody of very young children to the mother. If one of the parents has an illness that may impair the ability to parent, it may be considered by the court. Similarly, the judge may look at special health needs of a child.

Effect on the Child of Continuing or Disrupting an Existing Relationship. This factor might be applied in your case if you stayed at home for a period of years to care for your child, and awarding custody to the other parent would disrupt your relationship with your child.

Attitude and Stability of Each Parent's Character. The court may consider your ability and willingness to be cooperative with the other parent in deciding who should be awarded custody. The court may also consider each parent's history, which reflects the stability of his or her character.

Moral Fitness of Each Parent, Including Sexual Conduct. The extent to which a judge assesses the morals of a parent can vary greatly from judge to judge. Your own sexual conduct is ordinarily not considered unless it has harmed your child or your child was exposed to such sexual conduct.

Capacity to Provide Physical Care and Satisfy Educational Needs. Here the court may examine whether you or the other parent is better able to provide for your child's daily needs such as nutrition, health care, hygiene, social activities, and education. The court may also look to see whether you or your spouse has been attending to these needs in the past.

Preferences of the Child. The court must consider the preference of a child who is twelve years of age or older. The court may hear the preference of a younger child upon request. The preferences of older children will normally be given greater weight than those of younger children.

Health, Welfare, and Social Behavior of the Child. Every child is unique. Your child's needs must be considered when it comes to deciding custody and parenting time. The custody of a child with special needs, for example, may be awarded to the parent who is better able to meet those needs.

The judge may also consider whether you or your spouse has fulfilled the role of primary care provider for meeting the child's day-to-day needs.

Domestic Violence. Domestic violence is an important factor in determining custody, parenting time, and protection from abuse during the transfer of your child to the other parent. If domestic violence is a concern in your case, be sure to discuss it in detail with your attorney during the initial consultation so every measure can be taken to protect the safety of you and your children.

8.3 What's the difference between *visitation* and *parenting time*?

Historically, time spent with the noncustodial parent was referred to as *visitation*. Today, the term *parenting time* is used to refer to the time a child spends with either parent.

This change in language reflects the intention that children spend time with both parents and have two homes, as opposed to their living with one parent and visiting the other.

8.4 How can I make sure I will get to keep the children during the divorce proceedings?

You cannot ensure that your children will stay with you during the divorce process. However, the best way to provide clarity about the living arrangements and respective parenting time with your children during your divorce is to obtain a temporary order. Informal agreements between parties cannot always be trusted. Additionally, informal agreements with your spouse lack the ability to be enforced by the court. Thus, even if you and your spouse have agreed to temporary arrangements, talk with your attorney about whether this agreement should be formalized in a court order.

Obtaining a temporary order can be an important protection not only for the custody of your children, but also for other issues such as support, temporary exclusive possession of the marital home, temporary protection from your spouse, and attorney's fees.

Until a temporary order is entered, it's best that you continue to reside with your children. If you are considering leaving your home, talk with your attorney before making any significant changes to your living situation. If you must leave your home, take your children with you and talk with your attorney at your earliest opportunity.

8.5   How much weight does the child's preference carry?
The preference of your child is only one of many factors a judge may consider in determining custody. The age of your child and his or her ability to express the underlying reason for their preference will determine the amount of weight a judge will give to this preference. At the age of twelve, a child has the right to voice his or her preference as far as a parenting schedule. Although, not controlling, a judge will consider the preferences. Generally, the older the child is, the more weight the judge will give to the preference.

The reasoning underlying your child's preference is also a factor to consider. Consider the fifteen-year-old girl who wants to live with her mother because "Mom lets me stay out past curfew, I get a bigger allowance, and I don't have to do chores." Greater weight might be given to the preference of an eight-year-old who wants to live with his mother because "she helps me with my homework, reads me bedtime stories, and doesn't call me names like Dad does."

If you see that your child's preference may be a factor in the determination of custody, discuss it with your lawyer so that this consideration is a part of assessing the action to be taken in your case.

8.6   How old do the children have to be before they can speak to the judge about with whom they want to live?
At age twelve, a court has to listen to a preference from a child. Some judges will also hear from younger children. If either you or your spouse wants the judge to listen to what your child has to say, the request is ordinarily made to the judge to have the child speak to the judge in the judge's office (chambers) rather than from the witness stand. Depending upon the judge's decision, the attorneys for you and your spouse may also be present.

It is possible that the judge may also allow the attorneys to question the child. If you have concerns about the other parent learning what your child says to the judge, talk to your lawyer about the possibility of obtaining a directive from the court to keep this information confidential.

Typically, the testimony of the child is made "on the record," meaning, in the presence of a court reporter. This is so the testimony can be transcribed later in the event of an appeal.

In addition to the age of a child, a judge may consider such facts as the child's maturity and personality in determining whether a private interview of the child by the judge will be helpful to the custody decision-making process.

8.7   How can I prove that I was the primary care provider?

One tool to assist you and your attorney in establishing your case as a primary care provider is a chart indicating the care you and your spouse have each provided for your child. The clearer you are about the history of parenting, the better job your attorney can do in presenting your case to the judge.

Look at the activities in the chart to help you review the role of you and your spouse as care providers for your child.

Sample Parental Caregiving Chart

Activity	Mother	Father
Attended prenatal medical visits	———	———
Attended prenatal class	———	———
Took time off work after child was born	———	———
Got up with child at feedings	———	———
Got up with child when sick at night	———	———
Bathed child	———	———
Put child to sleep	———	———
Potty-trained child	———	———
Prepared and fed meals to child	———	———
Helped child learn numbers, letters, colors, etc.	———	———
Helped child with practice for music, dance lessons, sports	———	———
Took time off work for child's appointments	———	———
Stayed home from work with sick child	———	———
Took child to doctor visits	———	———
Went to pharmacy for child's medication	———	———
Administered child's medication	———	———
Took child to therapy	———	———

Child Custody

Activity	Mother	Father
Took child to optometrist	____	____
Took child to dentist	____	____
Took child to get haircuts	____	____
Bought clothing for child	____	____
Bought school supplies for child	____	____
Transported child to school	____	____
Picked up child after school	____	____
Drove carpool for child's school	____	____
Went to child's school activities	____	____
Helped child with homework and projects	____	____
Attended parent-teacher conferences	____	____
Helped in child's classroom	____	____
Chaperoned child's school trips	____	____
Transported child to day care	____	____
Communicated with day care providers	____	____
Transported child from day care	____	____
Attended day care activities	____	____
Signed child up for sports, dance, music	____	____
Bought equipment for sports, dance, music	____	____
Transported child to sports, dance, music	____	____
Attended sports, music, dance recitals	____	____
Coached child's sports	____	____
Transported child from sports, dance, music	____	____
Knows child's friends and friend's families	____	____
Took child to religious education	____	____
Participated in child's religious education	____	____
Obtained information and training about special needs of child	____	____
Comforted child during times of emotional upset	____	____

8.8 Do I have to let my spouse see the children before we are actually divorced?

Unless your children are at risk for being harmed by your spouse, your children should maintain regular contact with the other parent. It is important for children to experience the presence of both parents in their lives, regardless of the separation of the parents. Even if there is no temporary order for parenting time, cooperate with your spouse in making reasonable arrangements for time with your children. When safety is not an issue, if you deny contact with the other parent prior to trial, your judge is likely to question whether you have the best interests of your child at heart. Talk to your spouse or your lawyer about what parenting time schedule would be best for your children on a temporary basis.

8.9   I am seeing a therapist. Will that hurt my chances of getting custody?

If you are seeing a therapist, commend yourself for getting the professional support you need. Your well-being is important to your ability to be the best parent you can be.

Discuss with your lawyer the implications of your being treated by a therapist. It may be that the condition for which you are being treated in no way affects your child or your ability to be a loving and supportive parent.

Your mental health records may be subpoenaed by the other parent's lawyer. For this reason it is important to discuss with your attorney an action plan for responding to a request to obtain records in your therapist's file. Ask your attorney to contact your therapist to alert him or her regarding how to respond to a request for your mental health records.

8.10   I am taking prescription medication to treat my depression. Will this hurt my chances of getting custody?

No. Feelings of depression, anxiety, and trouble sleeping are common during a divorce. If you have any mental health concerns, seek help from a professional. Following through with the recommendations made by your health care provider, including the use of prescription medication, will be looked upon favorably by the court.

8.11   Will my children be present if we go to court?

In most instances, no. Judges make every effort to protect minor children from the conflict of their parents. For this reason, most judges will not allow children to be present in the courtroom to hear the testimony of other witnesses.

Although the risk that your spouse may share information with your child cannot be eliminated, it would be highly unusual for a judge to allow a child to hear testimony in a courtroom.

8.12   Should I hire a private detective to prove my spouse is having an affair?

If custody is disputed and your spouse is having an affair, discuss with your attorney how a private investigator might help you gather evidence to support your case. Discuss the following considerations with your attorney:

- How is the affair affecting the children?
- How much will a private investigator cost?
- Will the evidence gathered help my case?

Your attorney can help you determine whether hiring a private investigator is a good idea in your particular case.

8.13   Will the fact that I had an affair during the marriage hurt my chances of getting custody?

Whether an affair will have any impact on your custody case depends upon many factors, including:

- Whether the children were exposed to the affair
- Whether the affair had any emotional impact on the children
- How long ago the affair occurred
- The quality of the evidence about the affair

In determining custody, a court may consider the parent's moral fitness, which includes his or her sexual activity. However, these considerations will only be taken into account if the children were exposed to sexual activity or were adversely affected by the exposure to an affair. If you had an affair during your marriage, discuss it with your attorney at the outset so that you can assess its impact, if any, on custody.

8.14   During the months it takes to get a divorce is it okay to date or will it hurt my chances at custody?

If custody is disputed, talk with your attorney about your plans to begin dating. Your dating may be irrelevant if the children are unaware of it. However, most judges will frown upon exposing your children to a new relationship when they are still adjusting to the separation of their parents.

If your spouse is contesting custody, it may be best to focus your energy on your children, the litigation, and taking care of yourself.

If you do date and become sexually involved with your new partner, it is imperative that your children not be exposed to any sexual activity. If they are, it could harm your case for custody.

8.15 Can having a live-in partner hurt my chances of getting custody?

If you are contemplating having your new partner live with you, discuss your decision with your attorney first. If you are already living with your partner, let your attorney know right away so that the potential impact on any custody ruling can be assessed.

Your living with someone who is not your spouse may have significant impact on your custody case. However, judges' opinions of the significance of this factor can vary greatly. Talk promptly and frankly with your lawyer. It will be important for you to look together at many factors, including the following:

- How the judge assigned to your case views this situation
- Whether your living arrangement is likely to prompt a custody dispute that would not otherwise arise
- How long you have been separated from the other parent
- How long you have been in a relationship with your new partner
- The history and nature of the children's relationship with your partner
- Your future plans with your partner (such as marriage)

Living with a partner may put your custody case at risk. Consider such a decision thoughtfully, taking account the advice of your lawyer.

8.16 Can I have witnesses speak on my behalf to try to get custody of my children?

Absolutely. Witnesses are critical in every custody case. At a trial for the final determination of custody, you and the other parent will each have an opportunity to present witnesses who will give live testimony on your behalf.

Among those you might consider as potential witnesses in your custody case are:

- Family members
- Family friends
- Child-care providers
- Neighbors
- Teachers
- Health care providers
- Clergy members

In determining which witnesses would best support your case, your attorney may consider the following:

- What is the witness's opportunity to observe you or the other parent, especially with your child?
- How frequently? How recently?
- How long has the witness known you or the other parent?
- What is the relationship of the witness to the child and the parents?
- How valuable is the knowledge that this witness has?
- Does this witness have knowledge different from that of other witnesses?
- Is the witness available and willing to testify?
- Is the witness clear in conveying information?
- Is the witness credible, that is, will the judge believe this witness?
- Does the witness have any biases or prejudices that could impact the testimony?

You and your attorney can work together to determine which witnesses will best support your case. Support your attorney by providing a list of potential witnesses together with your opinion regarding the answers to the above questions.

Give your attorney the phone numbers, addresses, and workplaces of each of your potential witnesses. This information can be critical to the role that the attorney has in interviewing the witnesses, contacting them regarding testifying, and issuing subpoenas to compel their court attendance if needed. When parents give conflicting testimony during a custody trial, the testimony of other witnesses can be key to determining the outcome of the case.

8.17   Will my attorney want to speak with my children?

In most cases your attorney won't ask to speak with your children. An exception might be where custody is disputed or where either parent has made allegations of abuse or neglect. Your attorney may wish to speak to your child if he or she is older and has a preference regarding the parent who he or she wishes to live with primarily.

Not all attorneys are trained in appropriate interviewing techniques for children, especially for younger children. If the attorney has not spent a lot of time with children or is not familiar with child development, the interview may not provide meaningful information. Don't hesitate to ask your attorney about his or her experience in working with children before you agree to an interview of your child.

If your attorney asks to meet with your child, provide some background information about your child first. Let your attorney know your child's personality, some of his or her interests, and any topics that might upset your child. This background will help the attorney exercise the care essential any time a professional questions a child.

If you are concerned that going to your attorney's office for an interview will cause undue anxiety for your child, ask your attorney whether the interview can take place in a setting that would be more comfortable for your child. This might be a public place or your home.

8.18   How might photographs or a video of my child help my custody case?

Photographs or a video depicting your child's day-to-day life can help the judge learn more about your child's needs. It can demonstrate how your child interacts with you, with siblings, and with other important people in your family's life. The photographs or video can portray your child's room, home, and neighborhood, as well as show your child participating in activities.

Talk to your attorney about whether photographs or a video would be helpful in your case. Although photographs are more commonly used and are typically sufficient evidence, ask your lawyer if he or she recommends making a video, and if so, what scenes to include, the length of the video, keeping the original tapes, and the editing process.

8.19   What does it mean to be an *unfit* parent?

Parental *unfitness* means you have a personal deficiency or incapacity that will likely prevent you from performing essential parental obligations and is likely to result in a detriment to your child's well-being. Determinations of your fitness to be a custodial parent will largely depend upon the facts of your case. Reasons why a parent might be found to be unfit include a history of physical abuse, alcohol or drug abuse, or mental health problems that affect the ability to parent.

8.20   If I am awarded shared parenting time, what are some examples of how the parenting time might be shared?

In shared parenting arrangements, many parents follow a 2-2-3 schedule, or a variation thereof, whereby one parent has the child for two weekdays, the other parent has the child for the following two weekdays, and then the child goes back to the first parent for a three-day weekend. An sample parenting chart to demonstrate the 2-2-3 schedule appears on the following page.

Sample 2-2-3 Parenting Time Schedule

	Monday	Tuesday	Wednesday	Thursday	Friday	Saturday	Sunday
Week 1	Mother at 8 A.M.	Mother	Father Beginning at 5:00 P.M.	Father	Mother Beginning at 5:00 P.M.	Mother	Mother
Week 2	Father at 8 A.M.	Father	Mother Beginning at 5:00 P.M.	Mother	Father Beginning at 5:00 P.M.	Father	Father

Some parents prefer to have a one-week-on, one-week-off parenting schedule. However, this is not always preferred by the courts because the child is away from the other parent for such an extended period of time. Talk with your attorney about other possibilities as each situation is unique.

8.21 If my spouse is awarded custody of our child, how much time will our child spend with me?

Parenting time schedules for noncustodial parents vary from case to case. However, historically, the standard parenting time schedule for noncustodial parents is alternating weekends and one evening during the week. Additionally, holidays are alternated between the parents and Mother's Day and Father's Day are spent with the appropriate parent. Holiday parenting time supersedes the regular weekly schedule for parenting time. As in the determination of custody, the best interests of the child are what a court considers in determining the parenting time schedule. Among the factors that can impact a parenting time schedule are the past history of parenting time, the age and needs of the child, and the parents' work schedules.

If you and your spouse are willing to reach your own agreement about the parenting time schedule, you are likely to be more satisfied with it than with one imposed by a judge. Because you and your spouse know your child's needs, your family traditions, and your personal preferences, you can design a plan uniquely suited to your child's best interests.

If you and your spouse are unable to reach an agreement on a parenting time schedule, either on your own or with the assistance of your lawyers or a mediator, the judge will decide the schedule.

Child Custody

8.22 How is decision making authority decided?

The parent who is awarded custody has decision-making authority and the responsibility and authority to make all fundamental decisions regarding the child's welfare. Examples of fundamental decisions include, but are not limited to issues such as religion, education, extracurricular activities and non-emergency medical treatment. You can be awarded either sole or joint role legal custody.

If you are awarded custody, you have the sole authority to make fundamental decisions for your child, such as what school your child will attend, who your child's treating physician will be, and whether your child should undergo elective treatments or surgeries. However, even if you are awarded custody, your former spouse still has the authority and responsibility to make the day-to-day decisions for your child when he or she is in the other parent's care.

If you are awarded joint custody, decision-making authority is shared. This necessitates that both parents be able to communicate and agree upon fundamental decisions regarding the children. You might be good candidates for joint custody if you share a mutual respect for each other, you are able to communicate effectively, and you are able to cooperate and work together in a co-parenting relationship.

If you share custody and are unable to reach agreement on a major decision, such as a child's school or child-care provider, you may be required to return to mediation or to court to resolve your dispute. This can lead to delays in matters important to your child, increased conflict, and more legal fees.

However, it is unlikely the court will award joint legal custody if you and your spouse disagree about the fundamental decisions regarding your child's welfare, or if you are unable to be consistent and support each other in decisions regarding your children. Additionally, if domestic violence has been present in the marriage it is unlikely that the court will award joint legal custody.

8.23 What does it mean to have *split custody*?

Split custody refers to a custodial arrangement whereby each parent has sole physical custody of one or more of the children. Courts generally disfavor split custody because it

113

separates the children from each other. However, in families with a disabled child, or a child who is in need of additional health services, the use of split custody can provide for more attention and care focused upon the child in need.

8.24   I am concerned about protecting my child from abuse by my spouse. Which types of past abuse by my spouse are important to tell my attorney?

Keeping your child safe is your top priority. For your attorney to help you protect your child, provide a full history of the following:

- Hitting, kicking, pushing, shoving, or slapping you or your child
- Sexual abuse
- Threats to harm you or the child
- Threats to abduct your child
- Destruction of property
- Torture or harm to pets
- Requiring your child to keep secrets

The process of writing down past events may help you to remember other incidents of abuse you had forgotten. Be as complete as possible.

8.25   I don't think it's safe for my children to have any contact with my spouse. How can I prove this to the judge?

Keeping your children safe is of such importance that you should talk with your attorney immediately about a plan for the protection of you and your children. Options include a protection order, supervised visitation, or certain restrictions on your spouse's parenting time, such as no overnight visitation.

Make sure you have an attorney who understands your concerns for the welfare of your children. If your attorney is not taking your worry about the safety of your children seriously, you may be better served by a lawyer with a greater understanding of the issues in your case.

Give your attorney a complete history of the facts upon which you base your belief that your children are not safe with the other parent. Although the most recent facts are often the most relevant, it is important that your attorney have a clear picture of the background as well.

Your attorney also needs information about your spouse, such as whether your spouse is or has been:

- Using alcohol or drugs
- Treated for alcohol or drug use
- Arrested, charged, or convicted of crimes of violence
- Subject to a protection order for harassment or violence

8.26 How can I get my spouse's parenting time to be supervised?

If you are concerned about the safety of your children when they are with your spouse, talk to your lawyer. It may be that a protection order is warranted to terminate or limit contact with your children. Alternatively, it is possible to ask the judge to consider certain court orders intended to better protect your children.

Ask your attorney whether, under the facts of your case, the judge would consider any of the following court orders:

- Supervised visits
- Exchanges of the children in a public place
- Parenting class for the other parent
- Anger management or other rehabilitative program for the other parent

8.27 My spouse keeps saying he will get custody because there were no witnesses to his abuse and I can't prove it. Is he right?

No. Most domestic violence is not witnessed by others, and judges know this. If you have been a victim of abusive behavior by your spouse, or if you have witnessed your children as victims, your testimony is likely to be the most compelling evidence.

Be sure to tell your attorney about anyone who may have either seen your spouse's behavior or spoken to you or your children right after an abusive incident. They may be important witnesses in your custody case.

8.28   What documents or items should I give my attorney to help prove the history of domestic violence by my spouse?

The following may be useful exhibits if your case goes to court:

- Photographs of injuries
- Photographs of damaged property
- Abusive or threatening notes, letters, texts, or e-mails
- Abusive or threatening voice messages
- Your journal entries about abuse
- Police reports
- Medical records
- Court records
- Criminal and traffic records
- Damaged property, such as torn clothing

Tell your attorney which of these items you have or are able to obtain. Ask your attorney whether others can be acquired through a subpoena or other means.

8.29   I want to talk to my spouse about our child, but all she wants to do is argue. How can I communicate without it always turning into a fight?

Because conflict is high between you and your spouse, consider the following:

- Ask your attorney to help obtain a court order for custody and parenting time that is specific and detailed. A quality parenting plan lowers the amount of necessary communication between you and your spouse.
- Consider using e-mail or mail, especially for less urgent communication with your spouse.
- Avoid criticisms of your spouse's parenting.
- Avoid telling your spouse how to parent.

- Be factual and business-like when dealing with your spouse.
- Acknowledge to your spouse the good parental qualities he or she displays, such as being concerned, attentive, or generous.
- Keep your child out of any conflicts.

By focusing on your behavior, conflict with your spouse has the potential to decrease. Additionally, talk to your attorney about developing a communication protocol to follow when communicating with your spouse.

8.30 What if the child is not returned from parenting time at the agreed-upon time? Should I call the police?

Calling the police should be done only as a last resort if you feel that your child is at risk for abuse or neglect, or if you have been advised by your attorney that such a call is warranted. The involvement of law enforcement officials in parental conflict can result in far greater trauma to a child than a late return at the end of a parenting time.

The appropriate response to a child not being returned according to a court order depends upon the circumstances. If the problem is a recurring one, talk to your attorney regarding your options. It may be that a change in the schedule would be in the best interests of your child.

Regardless of the behavior of the other parent, make every effort to keep your child out of any conflicts between the adults.

8.31 If I have custody, may I move out of state without the permission of the court?

No. A custodial parent must obtain permission of the court prior to moving out of state with a child. If your former spouse agrees to your move, contact your attorney for preparing and submitting the necessary documents to your former spouse and the court for approval. Likewise, a move of over fifty miles requires court approval.

If your former spouse objects to your move, you must apply to the court for permission, and you will have a trial for the judge to decide.

To obtain the court's permission, you must first prove that you have a legitimate reason for the move, such as a better job or a transfer of your new spouse's employment. You must also prove that the move is in the best interests of your child. Temporary removal of a child in such cases is ordinarily not granted. It may be important to expedite your case so you will have a final court ruling determining whether you may move out of state with your child.

8.32 If I am not given custody, what rights do I have regarding medical records and medical treatment for my child?

Regardless of which parent has custody, state law allows both parents to have access to the medical records of their children and to make emergency medical decisions.

8.33 If I don't have custody, how will I know what's going on at my child's school?

Regardless of your custodial status, you have a right to have access to your child's school records.

Develop a relationship with your child's teachers and the school staff. Request to be put on the school's mailing list for all notices. Find out what is necessary for you to do to get copies of important school information and report cards.

Communicate with the other parent to both share and receive information about your child's progress in school. This will enable you to support your child and one another through any challenging periods of your child's education. It also enables you to share a mutual pride in your child's successes.

Regardless of which parent has custody, your child will benefit by your involvement in his or her education through your participation in parent-teacher conferences, attendance at school events, help with school homework, and positive communication with the other parent.

8.34 If my spouse is awarded custody, can I still take my child to church during my parenting time?

Yes. The decision of which religion the child should be is a fundamental decision that is made by the parent who has custody. However, an noncustodial parent retains the authority to make day-to-day decisions for the child while he or she is in their care. This means that an noncustodial parent can still take their child to church or participate in religious activities during their parenting time.

8.35 What if my child does not want to visit the other parent? Can my former spouse force the child to go?

If your child resists going with the other parent, it can first be helpful to determine the underlying reason. Consider these questions:

- What is your child's stated reason for not wanting to go?
- Does your child appear afraid, anxious, or sad?
- Do you have any concerns regarding your child's safety while with the other parent?
- Have your prepared your child for being with the other parent, speaking about the experience with enthusiasm and encouragement?
- Is it possible your child perceives your anxiety about the situation and is consequently having the same reaction?
- Have you provided support for your child's transition to the other home, such as completing fun activities in your home well in advance of the other parent's starting time?
- Have you spoken to the other parent about your child's behavior?
- Can you provide anything to ensure your child's time with the other parent is comfortable, such as a favorite toy or blanket?
- Have you established clear routines that support your child to be ready to go with the other parent with ease, such as packing a backpack or saying good-bye to a family pet?

The reason for a child's reluctance to go with the other parent may be as simple as being sad about leaving you or as serious as being a victim of abuse in the other parent's home. It is important to look at this closely to determine the best response.

Judges treat compliance with court orders for parenting time seriously. If one parent believes that the other is intentionally interfering with parenting time or the parent-child relationship, it can result in further litigation. At the same time, you want to know that your child is safe. Talk with your attorney about the best approach in your situation.

8.36   What steps can I take to prevent my spouse from getting the children in the event of my death?

Unless the other parent is not fit to have custody, he or she will have first priority as the guardian of your child in the event of your death. All parents should have a will naming a guardian for their children. In the event you do not intend to name the other parent, talk with your attorney. Seek counsel about how to best document and preserve the evidence that will be needed to prove that the other parent is unfit to have custody in the event of your death.

9

Child Support

Whether you will be paying or receiving child support may be the subject of much worry. Will you receive enough support to take care of your children? Will you have enough money to live on after you pay child support? How will you make ends meet?

Most parents want to provide for their children. Today, the child support laws make it possible for parents to have a better understanding of their obligation to support their children. The mechanisms for both payment and receipt of child support are more clearly defined, and help is available for collecting support if it's not paid.

The Tennessee Child Support Guidelines, the Child Support Payment Center, and the Child Support Receipting Unit all help to simplify the child support system. As you learn more about them, matters regarding child support that appeared complex in the beginning can eventually become routine for you and the other parent.

9.1   What determines whether I will get child support?

Whether you will receive child support depends upon a number of factors. These may include how much time your child is living in your household, which parent has custody, and each parent's income.

If you have physical custody of your child, it is likely your spouse will be ordered to pay support for any children born or adopted during your marriage.

121

9.2   Can I get temporary support while waiting for custody to be decided?

A judge has authority to enter a temporary order for a parenting plan and child support. This order ordinarily remains in place until a final decree establishing custody is entered. In most cases, a hearing for temporary custody and support can be held shortly after the filing for divorce.

9.3   What is *temporary support* and how soon can I get it?

Temporary support is paid for the support of a spouse or a child. It is paid sometime after the divorce complaint is filed and continues until your final decree of divorce is entered by the court or until your case is dismissed.

If you are in need of temporary support, talk to your attorney at your first opportunity. If you and your spouse are unable to agree on the amount of temporary support to be paid each month, talk to your attorney. If an agreement is not reached, it is likely that your attorney will file a motion for temporary support, asking the judge to decide how much the support should be and when it will start.

Because there are a number of steps to getting a temporary child-support order, don't delay in discussing your need for support with your lawyer. Child support will not be ordered for any period prior to the filing of a request for it with the court.

The following are the common steps in the process:

- You discuss your need for a temporary child support with your lawyer.
- Your lawyer requests a hearing date from the judge and prepares the necessary documents.
- A temporary hearing is held and child support is ordered.
- The temporary order is signed by the judge.

If your spouse is not paying you support voluntarily, time is of the essence in obtaining a temporary order for support. This should be one of the first issues you discuss with your lawyer.

9.4 How soon does my spouse have to start paying support for the children?

Your spouse may begin paying you support voluntarily at any time. A temporary order for support will give you the right to collect the support if your spouse stops paying. Talk to your lawyer about court hearings for temporary support in your county.

9.5 How is the amount of child support I'll receive or pay figured?

The Tennessee Child Support Guidelines set forth the standards by which your child support is calculated. According to the guidelines, both parents have a duty to contribute to the support of their children in proportion to their respective net incomes. As a result, both your income and the income of your spouse will factor into the child-support calculation.

Other factors the court may consider include:

- The additional cost of health insurance for the child
- Regularly paid support for other children
- Work-related day care expenses for the child

Child support that is higher or lower than what the guidelines provide for may be awarded in certain cases, for example:

- When either parent or child has extraordinary medical costs
- When a child is disabled with special needs
- When juveniles are placed in foster care
- Whenever the application of the guidelines in an individual case would be unjust or inappropriate

When a judge orders an amount of support that is different from the guideline amount, it is referred to as a *deviation.*

9.6 Will the type of custody arrangement or the amount of parenting time I have impact the amount of child support I receive?

It can. Sharing physical custody can dramatically lower child-support amounts and, in lieu of child support, an expense-sharing arrangement may be ordered. For this reason, it is essential that you discuss child support with your attorney prior to reaching any agreements with your spouse regarding custody or parenting time.

If you intend to mediate custody or parenting time, be sure to talk with your attorney in advance regarding how it can affect your child support.

9.7 Is overtime pay considered in the calculation of child support?

Yes, if your overtime is a routine part of your employment that you can actually expect to earn regularly. The judge can consider your work history, the degree of control you have over your overtime, and the nature of the field in which you work.

9.8 Will rental income be factored into my child support, or just my salary?

Income from other sources may be considered in determining the amount of child support.

9.9 My spouse has a college degree but refuses to get a job. Will the court consider this in determining the amount of child support?

The earning capacity of your spouse may be considered instead of their current income. The court can look at your spouse's work history, education, skills, health, and job opportunities.

If you believe your spouse is earning substantially less than the income she or he is capable of earning, provide your attorney with details. Ask about making a case for child support based on earning capacity instead of actual income.

9.10 Will I get the child support directly from my spouse or from the state?

It can be from either. Generally, it works best for each party for the support to be deducted from the obligor spouse's wages. A record is kept by the Tennessee Child Support Receipting Unit of all payments that are made. However, it is acceptable for payments to be made directly between the parents. In those cases, it is important that such payment be made by check or money order and a record of the payments be kept.

9.11 How soon can I expect my child-support payments to start arriving?

A number of factors may affect the date on which you will begin receiving your child support. Here are the usual steps in the process:

- A child-support amount and start date for the support are decided either by agreement between you and your spouse or by the judge.
- Either your attorney or your spouse's attorney prepares the court order.
- The attorney who did not write the court order reviews and approves it.
- The court order is taken to the judge for signature.
- Your spouse signs a Notice to Withhold Income form and delivers it to his or her employer, asking that child support be withheld from future paychecks.
- Your spouse's employer withholds the support from the paycheck.
- The child support is transferred by the employer into the Tennessee Child Support Payment Center.
- The Payment Center sends the money to you, either by direct deposit or mail.

As you can see, there are a lot of steps in this process. Plan your budget knowing that the initial payment of child support might be delayed.

9.12 Will some amount of child support be withheld from every paycheck?

It depends on the employer's policy and how employees are paid. If support is due on the first of the month, the employer has the full month to withhold the amount ordered to be paid. If an employer issues paychecks twice a month, it is possible that half of the support will be withheld from each check and paid in to the Tennessee Child Support Payment Center at the end of the month.

If an employer issues checks every other week, which is twenty-six pay periods per year, there will be some months in which a third paycheck is issued. Consequently, it is possible

125

that no child support will be withheld from the wages paid in that third check of the month, or that some checks will be for less than 50 percent of the monthly amount due.

Example: Suppose child support is $650 per month and the payor is paid every other Friday, or twenty-six times per year. The employer may withhold $300 per paycheck for child support. Although most months the support received will be $600, for a few months it will be $900. By the end of the year, however, the payor will have paid the same amount as if $650 had been paid each month.

Over time, child-support payments typically fall into a routine schedule which makes it easier for both the payor and the recipient to plan their budgets.

9.13 If my spouse has income other than from an employer, is it still possible to get a court order to withhold my child support from his income?

Yes. Child support can be automatically withheld from most sources of income. These may include unemployment, worker's compensation, retirement plans, and investment income.

9.14 Can I collect child support from both the biological parent and the adoptive parent of my child?

Possibly. When your child was adopted, the biological parent's duty to support your child ended. However, it may be possible for you to collect past due child support from the period of time before the adoption. The adoptive parent will have a duty to provide support upon your separation.

9.15 What happens with child support when our children go to the other parent's home for summer vacation? Is child support still due?

Yes, the child-support calculation takes into consideration all times with the child or children, including extended times.

9.16 What is a *child-support referee*?

Although it is likely that your child support will be decided by the judge hearing your divorce, in some jurisdictions, *child-support referees* are also authorized to hear matters regarding child support and spousal support. Referees are attorneys who are appointed to conduct hearings in the same manner as a judge.

After hearing the evidence, the referee will draw conclusions regarding the facts and make recommendations to the judge. The judge then has the authority to enter an order based upon the referee's written report.

If you are dissatisfied with the referee's findings and recommendations, talk to your attorney right away about filing an objection.

9.17   After the divorce, if I choose to live with my new partner rather than marry, can I still collect child support?

Yes. Although spousal support (alimony) may end if you live with your partner, child support does not terminate for this reason.

9.18   Can I still collect child support if I move to another state?

Yes. A move out of state will not end your right to receive child support. However, the amount of child support could be changed if other circumstances change, such as income or costs for exercising parenting time.

9.19   Can I expect to continue to receive child support if I remarry?

Yes. Your child support will continue even if you remarry.

9.20   How long can I expect to receive child support?

Under Tennessee law, child support is ordinarily ordered to be paid until the child graduates high school, reaches the age of eighteen—whichever occurs later—or dies.

9.21   Does interest accrue on past-due child support?

Yes, interest accrues on past-due child support at the rate of 12 percent annually.

9.22   What can I do if my former spouse refuses to pay child support?

The elected district attorney is responsible for enforcement of child support. All districts have attorneys who are specifically designated to perform child-support enforcement services. These attorneys are sometimes referred to as *authorized attorneys* or *child-support attorneys.*

If your former spouse is not paying child support, you may take action to enforce the court order either with the help of your lawyer or the assistance of a child-support attorney. Unlike a private attorney, you do not pay for the services of a child-support attorney.

The judge may order payment of both the current amount of support and an additional amount to be paid each month until the past-due child support (referred to as *arrearages*) is paid in full.

You may request that your former spouse's state and federal tax refunds be sent directly to the Tennessee Child Receipting Unit. It may also be possible to garnish a checking or savings account.

Driver's licenses may also be suspended if a parent falls behind in child-support payments. However, if there is a payment plan for the payment of arrearages, then licenses will not be suspended.

Your former spouse may also be found in contempt of court if the failure to pay support is intentional. Possible consequences include being fined or jailed.

To review, if you are not receiving child support, you have two options:

• Call your attorney.

• Visit your local district attorney's office.

9.23   At what point will the state help me collect back child support, and what methods do they use?

It depends. When the state will help you collect back child support and the methods they will use can depend upon the amount of back child support owed. You must initiate contact with the state if you want help in collecting your child support.

9.24   I live outside Tennessee. Will the money I spend on airline tickets to see my children impact my child support?

It might. If you expect to spend large sums of money for transportation in order to have parenting time with your children, talk to your attorney about how this might be taken into consideration when determining the amount of child support.

9.25   After the divorce, can my former spouse substitute buying sprees with the child for child-support payments?

No. Purchases of gifts and clothing for a child do not relieve your former spouse from an obligation to pay child support.

9.26   Are expenses such as child care supposed to be taken out of my child support?

The guidelines provide that each parent pay a percentage of the work, or school-related day care expenses in addition to the child support. It is figured into the child-support work sheet.

9.27   How does providing health insurance for my child affect my child-support amount?

If you pay the health insurance premium for your child, the amount you pay is taken into account when calculating child support. You will receive a credit for the amount you pay per month for your child's health insurance premium.

9.28   Am I required to pay for my child's uninsured medical expenses?

No. Each parent typically must pay a *pro rata* (in proportion or a prorated) share of uninsured medical expenses in accordance with his or her income.

9.29 Am I required to pay for general, everyday expenses for my child with the support I receive?

Yes, if you are receiving child support, under the guidelines you are responsible for expenses for your child such as housing, clothing, school lunches, and the cost for activities.

However, if you have a shared parenting arrangement, you may be required to participate in an expense-sharing arrangement with the other parent, where all reasonable and necessary expenses for your child, such as clothing and extracurricular activities, will be allocated between the parents.

9.30 Can my spouse be required by the decree to pay for our child's private elementary and high school education?

Probably not. The Tennessee Child Support Guidelines make no specific provision for private education tuition. However, some parents agree to include a provision in the decree for payment of such tuition because both parents believe it is important for their child.

If you want your spouse to share this expense for your child, talk it over with your lawyer. Be sure to provide your attorney with information regarding tuition, fees, and other expenses related to private education

9.31 Can my spouse be required by the decree to contribute financially to our child's college education?

The legal duty of a parent to support a child does not include payment for college education. However, if your spouse agrees to pay this expense, it can be included in the final decree and it will be an enforceable court order. Such a provision is ordinarily included in a divorce decree only as a result of a negotiated settlement.

If your decree includes a provision for payment of college education expenses, be sure it is specific. Terms to consider include:

- What expenses are included? For example, tuition, room and board, books, fees, travel, etc.
- Is there a limit? For example, up to the level of the cost of attendance at the University of Tennessee at Knoxville or a certain dollar amount.

- When is the payment due?
- For what period of time does it continue?
- Are there any limits on the type of education that will be paid for?

The greater the clarity in such a provision, the lower the risk is for misunderstanding or conflict years later.

10

Alimony

The mere mention of the word *alimony* might stir your emotions and start your stomach churning. If your spouse has filed for divorce and is seeking alimony, you might see it as a double injustice—your marriage is ending and you feel like you have to pay for it, too. If you are seeking alimony, you might feel hurt and confused that your spouse is resistant to help support you, even though you may have interrupted your career to stay home and care for your children.

Learning more about Tennessee's laws on alimony, also referred to as spousal support, can help you move from your emotional reaction to the reality of possible outcomes in your case. Uncertainty about the precise amount of alimony that may be awarded or the number of years it might be paid is not unusual. Work closely with your lawyer. Be open to possibilities. Try looking at it from your spouse's perspective.

With the help of your lawyer, you will know the best course of action to take toward an alimony decision you can live with after your divorce is over.

10.1   Which gets calculated first, child support or alimony?

Child support. Spousal support is determined from the income that is available after the amount of child support is determined.

Alimony

10.2 What's the difference between *spousal support* and *alimony*?

In Tennessee, *alimony* and *spousal support* have the same meaning.

10.3 How will I know if I am eligible to receive alimony?

Talk with your attorney about whether you are a candidate for alimony.

The opinions of Tennessee judges about awarding alimony vary greatly. Among the factors that may affect your eligibility to receive alimony are:

- The length of your marriage
- Your contributions to the marriage, including interruption of your career for the care of children or to support your spouse's career
- Your education, work history, health, income, and earning capacity
- Your overall financial situation compared to that of your spouse
- Your need for support
- Your spouse's ability to pay support

Every case for alimony is unique. Providing your lawyer with clear and detailed information about the facts of your marriage and current situation will allow him or her to make an alimony assessment in your case.

10.4 What information should I provide to my attorney if I want alimony?

If your attorney advises you that you may be a candidate for alimony, be sure to provide complete facts about your situation, including:

- A history of the interruptions in your education or career for the benefit of your spouse, including transfers or moves due to your spouse's employment
- A history of the interruptions in your education or career for raising children, including periods during which you worked part-time

- Your complete educational background, including the dates of your schooling or training and degrees earned
- Your work history, including the names of your employers, the dates of your employment, your duties, your pay, and the reasons you left
- Any pensions or other benefits lost due to the interruption of your career for the benefit of the marriage
- Your health history, including any current diagnoses, treatments, limitations, and medications
- Your monthly living expenses, including anticipated future expenses such as health insurance and tax on alimony
- A complete list of the debts for you and your spouse
- Income for you and your spouse, including all sources

Also include any other facts that might support your need for alimony, such as other contributions you made to the marriage, upcoming medical treatment, or a lack of jobs in the field in which you were formerly employed.

No two alimony cases are alike. The better the information your lawyer has about your situation, the easier it will be for him or her to assess your case for alimony

10.5   My spouse told me that because I had an affair during the marriage, I have no chance to get alimony even though I quit my job and have cared for our children for many years. Is it true that I have no case?

Not necessarily. Your right to alimony will be based on many factors, but having an affair is not an absolute bar to getting spousal support. However, if your affair had a financial impact on the marital estate, it may be taken into consideration when determining an award of alimony.

10.6   How is the amount of alimony calculated?

Unlike child support, there are not specific guidelines for determining the amount of alimony. A judge will look at the expenses and incomes of you and your spouse, after giving consideration to the payment and receipt of child support.

Judges are given a lot of discretion to make their own decision on alimony without the benefit of specific guidelines. Consequently, the outcome of an alimony ruling by a judge can be one of the most unpredictable aspects of your divorce.

10.7 My spouse makes a lot more money than he reports on our tax return, but he hides it. How can I prove my spouse's real income to show he can afford to pay alimony?

Alert your attorney to your concerns. Your lawyer can then take a number of actions to determine your spouse's income with greater accuracy. They are likely to include:

- More-thorough discovery
- An examination of check registers and bank deposits
- Inquiries about travel
- Depositions of third parties who have knowledge of income or spending by your spouse
- Subpoena of records of places where your spouse has made large purchases or received income
- Comparison of income claimed with expenses paid
- Inquiries of purchases made in cash

By partnering with your lawyer, you may be able to build a case to establish your spouse's actual income as greater than that shown on tax returns. If you filed joint tax returns, discuss with your lawyer any other implications of erroneous information on those returns.

10.8 What effect does spousal maintenance have on my taxes?

Most types of alimony are tax deductible for the payor and taxable income for the payee. You should consult with your accountant on any tax issue.

10.9 How is the purpose of alimony different from the payment of my property settlement?

Alimony and the division of property serve two distinct purposes, even though many of the factors for determining them are the same. The purpose of alimony is to provide support. In contrast, the purpose of a property division is to distribute the marital assets fairly between you and your spouse.

10.10 My spouse makes a lot more money than I do. Will I be awarded spousal maintenance to make up the difference in our income?

Although the purpose of alimony is to provide support, alimony awards are not used to equalize the incomes of the parties. Instead, alimony may be awarded to assist the economically disadvantaged spouse for the transitional period during and after the divorce, until he or she becomes economically self-sufficient. However, a disparity in income may be one factor the judge contemplates when considering an award of alimony.

10.11 How long can I expect to receive alimony?

Like your right to receive alimony, how long you will receive alimony will depend upon the facts of your case and the judge's philosophy toward alimony. In general, the longer your marriage, the stronger your case is for a long-term alimony award.

You may receive only temporary alimony, or you may receive alimony for several years. Talk to your attorney about the facts of your case to get a clearer picture of the possible outcomes in your situation. Unless you and your spouse agree otherwise, your alimony will automatically terminate upon your remarriage or the death of either of you.

10.12 Can remarriage affect my alimony?

Under Tennessee law, unless your divorce decree provides otherwise, alimony ends upon the remarriage of the recipient.

10.13 Does the death of my former spouse affect my alimony?

In most cases, yes. Under Tennessee law, unless your decree provides otherwise, alimony ends upon the death of either party.

10.14. Do I have to keep paying alimony if my former spouse is now living with a new significant other?

Yes. Do not stop making your alimony payments. Instead, contact your attorney to seek a modification of the alimony award. Support may be reduced or terminated with a new court order if your former spouse is living with a new significant other.

10.15 Can I continue to collect alimony if I move to a different state?

Yes. The duty of your former spouse to follow a court order to pay alimony does not end simply because you move to another state, unless this is a specific provision in your decree.

10.16 What can I do if my spouse stops paying alimony?

If your spouse stops paying alimony, see your attorney about your options for enforcing your court order. The judge may order the support be taken from a source of your spouse's income or from a financial account belonging to your spouse.

If your spouse is intentionally refusing to pay spousal support, talk to your attorney about whether pursuing a *contempt of court* action would be effective. In a contempt action, your spouse may be ordered to appear in court and provide evidence explaining why support has not been paid. Possible consequences for contempt of court include a jail sentence or a fine.

10.17 Can I return to court to modify alimony?

It depends. If your divorce decree provides that your alimony order is "non-modifiable," then it may not be modified. Also, your decree may not be modified to award alimony if alimony was not awarded in the original decree dissolving the marriage.

If there has been a material change in the circumstances of either you or your spouse, you may seek to have alimony modified. Examples include a serious illness or the loss or obtaining of a job.

A request to modify alimony for the purposes of seeking additional alimony may not be filed if the time for payment of alimony allowed under your original decree has already passed.

If you think you have a basis to modify your alimony, contact your attorney at once to be sure a timely modification request is filed with the court.

11

Division of Property

You never imagined that you would face losing the house you and your spouse so happily moved into—the house where you celebrated family traditions and spent countless hours making it "home." Your spouse wants it and your lawyer says it might have to be sold.

During a divorce, you will decide whether you or your spouse will take ownership of everything from bathroom towels to the stock portfolio. Suddenly you find yourself having a strong attachment to that lamp in the family room or the painting in the hallway. Why does the coin collection suddenly take on new meaning?

Do your best to reach agreement with your spouse regarding dividing household goods. Enlist the support of your attorney in deciding which assets should be valued by an expert, such as the family business or real estate. From tax consequences to replacement value, there are many factors to consider in deciding whether to fight to keep an asset, to give it to your spouse, or to have it sold.

Like all aspects of your divorce, take one step at a time. By starting with the items most easily divided, you and your spouse can avoid paying lawyers to litigate the value of that 1980s record album collection.

11.1 What system does Tennessee use for dividing property?

Tennessee law provides for an equitable or fair, but not necessarily equal, division of the property and debts acquired during your marriage.

Regardless of how title is held, the court can use its discretion to make a division of the marital assets and marital debts. In many cases this may mean an equal division, but as little as one-quarter of the assets awarded to one party and three-quarters to the other may still be considered "equitable."

The court will consider a number of factors, including your debts, the economic circumstances of you and your spouse, and the history of contributions to the marriage.

11.2 What does *community property* mean?

Community property is a term used in several states that have a community property system for dividing assets in a divorce. In states having community property laws, each spouse holds a one-half interest in most property acquired during the marriage. Because Tennessee is not a community property state, community property laws do not apply.

11.3 How is it determined who gets the house?

The first issue to be decided regarding the family home is the determination of who will retain possession of it while the divorce is pending. Later, it must be decided whether the house will be sold, or awarded to you or your spouse.

Several factors to consider when determining the disposition of the home are:

- Who can afford the mortgage and expenses associated with the home
- Who has custody of the children
- Whether the house is premarital
- Whether there are other assets in the marital estate to offset the value of the home

Consider the above factors and talk with your attorney about your options. If you and your spouse are unable to reach agreement regarding the house, the judge will decide who keeps it or whether it will be sold.

11.4   Should I sell the house during the divorce proceedings?

Selling your home is a big decision. To help you decide what is right for you, ask yourself these questions:

- What will be the impact on my children if the home is sold?
- Can I afford to stay in the house after the divorce?
- After the divorce, will I be willing to give the house and yard the time, money, and physical energy required for its maintenance?
- Is it necessary for me to sell the house to pay a share of the equity to my spouse, or are there other options?
- Would my life be easier if I were in a smaller or simpler home?
- Would I prefer to move closer to the support of friends and family?
- What is the state of the housing market in my community?
- What are the benefits of remaining in this house?
- Can I retain the existing mortgage or will I have to refinance?
- Will I have a higher or lower interest rate if I sell the house and buy a new one?
- Will I have the means to acquire another home?
- If I don't retain the home and my spouse asks for it, what effect will this have on my custody case?
- Will my spouse agree to the sale of the house?
- What will be the real estate commission?
- What will be the costs of preparing the house for sale?

Selling a home is more than just a legal or financial decision. When deciding whether to sell your home, consider what is important to you in creating your life after divorce.

11.5   How do I determine how much our house is worth?

In a divorce, the value of your home can be determined in a number of ways. You and your spouse can agree to the value of your home. You can seek advice from a local real estate agent on the approximate value of your home through a market analysis. Or, for a more authoritative valuation, you can hire a professional real estate appraiser to determine the value of your home. Talk to your attorney to determine the best method to value your home in your divorce.

11.6   My house is worth less than what is owed on the mortgage. What are my options?

Talk with your lawyer and consider consulting with a mortgage specialist. It is important to get an accurate assessment of the value of your house. Consider working with a professional, such as an appraiser or realtor, to obtain the estimated fair market value of your home. If your house is "underwater," meaning you owe more on the mortgage than your house is worth, you may decide to list your house for sale and keep it on the market while continuing to make your mortgage payments. Another option to consider is a short sale, where the lender accepts less money for your house than you owe. Seek advice from your lawyer and other financial experts to determine which option is best for you.

11.7   What is meant by *equity* in my home?

Regardless of who is awarded your house, the court will consider whether the spouse not receiving the house should be compensated for the equity in the house. *Equity* is the difference between the value of the home and the amount owed in mortgages against the property.

For example, if the first mortgage is $50,000 and the second mortgage from a home equity loan is $10,000, the total debt owed against the house is $60,000. If your home is valued at $100,000, the equity in your home is $40,000. (The $100,000 value less the $60,000 in mortgages equals $40,000 in equity.)

If one of the parties remains in the home, the issue of how to give the other party his or her share of the equity must be considered.

Division of Property

11.8   How will the equity in our house be divided?

If your home is going to be sold, the equity in the home will most likely be divided after the costs of the sale have been paid.

If either you or your spouse will be awarded the house, there are a number of options for the other party being compensated for his or her share of the equity in the marital home. These could include:

- The spouse who does not receive the house receives other assets (for example, retirement funds) to compensate for their respective share of the equity.

- The person who remains in the home agrees to refinance the home at some future date and to pay the other party his or her share of the equity.

- The parties agree that the property be sold at a future date, or upon the happening of a certain event such as the youngest child completing high school or the remarriage of the party keeping the home.

As the residence is often among the most valuable assets considered in a divorce, it is important that you and your attorney discuss the details of its disposition. These include:

- Valuation of the property
- Refinancing to remove a party from liability for the mortgage
- The dates on which certain actions should be taken, such as listing the home for sale
- The real estate agent
- Costs for preparing the home for sale
- Making mortgage payments

If you and your spouse do not agree regarding which of you will remain in the home, the court will decide who keeps it or may order the property sold.

11.9 If my spouse signs a *quitclaim deed*, does that remove his obligation to repay the mortgage?

No. A *quitclaim deed* is a legal document that transfers one person's interest in real property to another person. However, removing his name from the title of your property will not remove his obligation to repay the mortgage. You and your husband signed a contract with the lender to repay the debt you borrowed to purchase your home. To remove your husband from the obligation, you must seek a refinance of your current mortgage. A refinance involves obtaining a new mortgage loan to pay off the existing mortgage.

11.10 Who keeps all the household goods until the divorce decree is signed?

The court will ordinarily not make any decisions about who keeps the household goods on a temporary basis. Most couples attempt to resolve these issues on their own rather than incur legal fees to dispute household goods. However, the court will enter an order restraining the parties from transferring, selling, or destroying household goods during the divorce process, so that the goods remain intact and can be divided by the divorce decree.

11.11 How can I reduce the risk that assets will be hidden, transferred, or destroyed by my spouse?

Consulting with an attorney before filing for divorce can reduce the risk that assets will be hidden, transferred, or destroyed by your spouse. This is especially important if your spouse has a history of destroying property, incurring substantial debt, or transferring money without your knowledge.

These are among the possible actions you and your attorney can consider together:

- Placing your family heirlooms or other valuables in a safe location
- Transferring some portion of financial accounts prior to filing for divorce
- Preparing an inventory of the personal property
- Taking photographs or a video of the property

- Obtaining copies of important records or statements
- Obtaining a restraining order before your spouse is served with notice of the divorce

Plans to leave the marital home should also be discussed in detail with your attorney, so that any actions taken early in your case are consistent with your ultimate goals.

Speak candidly with your lawyer about your concerns so that a plan can be developed that provides a level of protection that is appropriate to your circumstances.

11.12 How are assets such as cars, boats, and furniture divided, and when does this happen?

In most cases, spouses are able to reach their own agreements about how to divide personal property, such as household furnishings and vehicles.

If you and your spouse disagree about how to divide certain items, it can be wise to consider which are truly valuable to you, financially or otherwise. Perhaps some of them can be easily replaced. Always look to see whether it is a good use of your attorney fees to argue over items of personal property. If a negotiated settlement cannot be reached, the issue of the division of your property will be made by the judge at trial.

11.13 How do I value our used personal property?

In a divorce, your personal property will be valued at its fair market value. The *fair market value* is the price a buyer would be willing to pay for the item at a garage sale or on an online auction website. For example, if you bought a sofa for $1,000 five years ago, the fair market value of the couch is what you could sell it for at a garage sale today. The fair market value is not how much the couch was when you bought it or how much it will cost to replace the couch. Instead, the value of your personal property is what you could reasonably sell it for in its current used condition.

11.14 My wife and I own a coin collection. How will our collection be valued and divided in our divorce?

If you own a unique collection, such as a gun, art, or coin collection, talk with your attorney about how to value the collection in your divorce. It may be that you will need the collection appraised by an expert who has specialized training and knowledge to determine its value. If you and your spouse cannot agree on who will keep the collection, it is possible the judge will order the collection to be sold or may order you to divide the collection between you and your spouse.

11.15 What is meant by a *property inventory* and how detailed should mine be?

A *property inventory* is a listing of the property you own. It may also include a brief description of the property. Discuss with your attorney the level of inventory detail needed to benefit your case.

Factors to consider when creating your inventory may include:

- The extent to which you anticipate you and your spouse will disagree regarding the division of your property
- Whether you anticipate a dispute regarding the value of the property either you or your spouse is retaining
- Whether you will have continued access to the property if a later inventory is needed or whether you spouse will retain control of the property
- Whether you or your spouse are likely to disagree about which items are premarital, inherited, or gifts from someone other than your spouse.

In addition to creating an inventory, your attorney may request that you prepare a list of the property that you and your spouse have already divided or a list of the items you want but your spouse has not agreed to give to you.

If you do not have continued access to your property, talk to your attorney about taking photographs or obtaining access to the property to complete your inventory.

11.16 What happens to our individual checking and savings accounts during and after the divorce?

Regardless of whose name is on the account, bank accounts may be considered marital assets and may be divided by the court. Discuss with your attorney the benefits of a temporary restraining order to protect bank accounts, how to retain access or obtain an accounting of these accounts, how to use these accounts while the case is pending, and the date on which financial accounts should be valued.

11.17 How and when are liquid assets like bank accounts and stocks divided?

Talk with your attorney early in your case about the benefits of a temporary restraining order to reduce the risk that your spouse will transfer money out of financial accounts or transfer other assets.

In many cases, couples will agree to divide bank accounts equally at the outset of the case. However, this may not be advisable in your case. Discuss with your attorney whether you should keep an accounting of how you spend money used from a bank account while your divorce is in progress.

Stocks are ordinarily a part of the final agreement for the division of property and debts. If you and your spouse cannot agree on how your investments should be divided, the judge will make the decision at trial.

11.18 How will our property in another state be divided?

For the purposes of dividing your assets, out-of-state property is treated the same as property in Tennessee. Although a Tennessee court cannot order a change in the title to property located in another state, a judge can order your spouse either to turn the property over to you or to sign a deed or other document to transfer title to you.

11.19 Are all of the assets—such as property, bank accounts, and inheritances—that I had prior to my marriage still going to be mine after the divorce?

It depends. In many cases the court will allow a party to retain an asset brought into the marriage, but the following are questions the court will consider in making its determination:

* Can the premarital asset be clearly traced? For example, if you continue to own a vehicle that you brought into the marriage, it is likely that it will be awarded to you as your separate property. However, if you brought a vehicle into the marriage, sold it during the marriage,

and spent the proceeds, it is less likely that the court will consider awarding you its value.

- Did you keep the property separate and titled in your name, or did you commingle it with marital assets? Premarital assets you kept separate may be more likely to be awarded to you.

- Did the other spouse contribute to the increase in the value of the premarital asset, and can the value of that increase be proven? For example, suppose a woman owned a home prior to her marriage. After the marriage, the parties lived in the home, continuing to make mortgage payments and improvements to the home. At the time of the divorce, the husband seeks a portion of the equity in the home. The court might consider the value of the home at the time of the marriage, any contributions to the increase in equity made by the husband, and the evidence of the value of those contributions.

11.20 Will I get to keep my engagement ring?

If your engagement ring was given to you prior to your marriage, it will be considered a gift and treated as premarital property that you can keep.

11.21 What does it mean to *commingle* property?

Commingling occurs when one spouse's separate property is mixed or combined with the marital property, such that the separate property can no longer be distinguished from the marital property.

11.22 Can I keep gifts and inheritances I received during the marriage?

Similar rules apply to gifts and inheritances received during the marriage as apply to premarital assets, that is, assets you owned prior to the marriage.

For gifts received during the marriage, such as a gift from a parent, the court will need to determine whether the gift was made to one party or to both. Whether you will be entitled to keep assets you inherited, assuming they are still in existence, will depend upon the unique circumstances of your case. When dividing the marital estate, the court may consider the fact that one spouse is allowed to keep substantial nonmarital assets such as an inheritance.

The following factors increase the probability that you will be entitled to keep your inheritance:

- It has been kept separate from the marital assets, such as a separate account.
- It is titled in your name only.
- It can be clearly identified.
- It has not been commingled with marital assets.
- Your spouse has not contributed to its care, operation, or improvement.

It is less likely that you will be awarded your full inheritance if:

- It was commingled with marital assets.
- Its origin cannot be traced.
- You have placed your spouse's name on the title.
- Your spouse has contributed to the increase in the value of the value of the inheritance.

If keeping your inheritance is important to you, talk to your attorney about the information needed to build your case.

11.23 If my spouse and I can't decide who gets what, who decides? Can that person's decision be contested?

If you and your spouse cannot agree on the division of your property, the judge will make the determination after considering the evidence at your trial.

If either party is dissatisfied with the decision reached by the judge, an appeal to a higher court is possible.

11.24 How are the values of property determined?

The value of some assets, like bank accounts, is usually not disputed. The value of other assets, such as homes or personal property, is more likely to be disputed.

If your case proceeds to trial, you may give your opinion of the value of property you own. You or your spouse may also have certain property appraised by an expert. In such cases it may be necessary to have the appraiser appear at trial to give testimony regarding the appraisal and the value of the asset.

If you own substantial assets for which the value is likely to be disputed, talk to your attorney early in your case about the benefits and costs of expert witnesses.

11.25 Who gets the interest from certificates of deposit, dividends from stock holdings, etc., during the divorce proceedings?

Whether you or your spouse receives interest from these assets is decided as a part of the overall division of your property and debts.

11.26 Does each one of our financial accounts have to be divided in half if we agree to an equal division of our assets?

No. Rather than incurring the administrative challenges and expense of dividing each asset in half, you and your spouse can decide that one of you will take certain assets equal to the value of assets taken by the spouse. If necessary, one of you can agree to make a cash payment to the other to make an equitable division.

11.27 Is my *health savings account* an asset that can be divided in the divorce?

Yes. A *health savings account (HSA)* is a tax-advantaged medical savings account to which contributions may be made by employees, employers, or both. Your HSA is an asset to be included in the property distribution and may be divided pursuant to your divorce decree and transferred to another HSA. A division pursuant to a decree does not constitute a distribution and is thus a tax-free transfer.

11.28 I worked very hard for years to support my family while my spouse completed an advanced degree. Do I have a right to any of my spouse's future earnings?

Your contributions during the marriage are a factor to be considered in both the division of the property and debts, as well as any award of alimony. Be sure to give your attorney a complete history of your contributions to the marriage and ask about their impact on the outcome of your case.

11.29 What factors determine whether I can get a share of my spouse's business?

Many factors determine whether you will get a share of your spouse's business and in what form you might receive it. Among the factors the court will look at are:

- Whether your spouse owned the business prior to your marriage
- Your role, if any, in operating the business or increasing its value
- The overall division of the property and debts

If you or your spouse owns a business, it is important that you work with your attorney early in your case to develop a strategy for valuing the business and making your case for how it should be treated in the division of property and debts.

11.30 My spouse and I have owned and run our own business together for many years. Can I be forced out of it?

Deciding what should happen with a family business when divorce occurs can be a challenge. Because of the risk for future conflict between you and your spouse, the value of the business is likely to be substantially decreased if you both remain owners.

In discussing your options with your lawyer, consider the following questions:

- If one spouse retains ownership of the business, are there enough other assets for the other spouse to receive a fair share of the total marital assets?
- Which spouse has the skills and experience to continue running the business?
- What would you do if you weren't working in the business?
- What is the value of the business?
- What is the market for the business if it were to be sold?

- Could you remain an employee of the business for some period of time even if you were not an owner?

You and your spouse know your business best. With the help of your lawyers, you may be able to create a settlement that can satisfy you both. If not, the judge will make the decision for you at trial.

11.31 I suspect my spouse is hiding assets, but I can't prove it. How can I protect myself if I discover later that I was right?

Ask your lawyer to include language in your divorce decree to address your concern. Insist that it include an acknowledgment by your spouse that the agreement was based upon a full and complete disclosure of your spouse's financial condition. Discuss with your lawyer a provision that allows for setting aside the agreement if it is later discovered that assets were hidden.

11.32 My spouse says I'm not entitled to a share of his stock options because he gets to keep them only if he stays employed with his company. What are my rights?

Stock options are often a very valuable asset. They are also one of the most complex issues when dividing assets during a divorce for these, among other, reasons:

- Each company has its own rules about awarding and exercising stock options.
- Complete information is needed from the employer.
- There are different methods for calculating the value of stock options.
- The reasons the options were given can impact the valuation and division. For example, some are given for future performance and may be considered separate property.
- There are cost and tax considerations when options are exercised.

Rather than being awarded a portion of the stock options themselves, you are likely to receive a share of the proceeds when the stock options are exercised.

If either you or your spouse owns stock options, begin discussing this asset with your attorney early in your case to allow sufficient time to settle the issues or to be well prepared for trial.

11.33 What is a *prenuptial agreement* and how might it affect the property settlement phase of the divorce?

A *prenuptial agreement,* sometimes referred to as a *premarital* or *antenuptial agreement,* is a contract entered into between two people prior to their marriage. It can include provisions for how assets and debts will be divided in the event the marriage is terminated, as well as provisions regarding spousal maintenance and attorney fees.

Your property settlement is likely to be impacted by the terms of your prenuptial agreement if the agreement is upheld as valid by the court.

11.34 Can a prenuptial agreement be contested during the divorce?

Yes. The court may consider many factors in determining whether to uphold your prenuptial agreement. Among them are:

- Whether your agreement was entered into voluntarily
- Whether your agreement was fair and reasonable at the time it was signed
- Whether you and your spouse gave a complete disclosure of your assets and debts
- Whether you and your spouse each had your own lawyer
- Whether you and your spouse each had enough time to consider the agreement

If you have a prenuptial agreement, bring a copy of it to the initial consultation with your attorney. Be sure to provide your lawyer with a detailed history of the facts and circumstances surrounding reaching and signing the agreement.

11.35 Will debts be considered when determining the division of the property?

Yes. The court will consider any debts incurred during the course of the marriage when dividing the property. For example, if you are awarded a car valued at $12,000, but you owe a $10,000 debt on the same vehicle, the court will take that debt into consideration in the overall division of the assets. Similarly, if one spouse agrees to pay substantial marital credit card debt, this obligation may also be considered in the final determination of the division of property and debts.

If your spouse incurred debts that you believe should be his or her sole responsibility, tell your attorney. Some debts may be considered nonmarital and treated separately from other debts incurred during the marriage. For example, if your spouse spent large sums of money on gambling or illegal drugs without your knowledge, you may be able to argue that those debts should be the sole responsibility of your spouse.

11.36 What is a *marital dissolution agreement*?

A *marital dissolution agreement* is a written document that includes all of the financial agreements you and your spouse have reached in your divorce. This may include the division of property, debts, child support, alimony, insurance, and attorney fees.

The property settlement may be a separate document, or it may be incorporated into the decree of dissolution, which is the final court order dissolving your marriage.

11.37 What happens after my spouse and I approve the marital dissolution agreement? Do we still have to go to court?

Not necessarily. After you and your spouse approve and sign the marital dissolution agreement or decree, it must still be approved by your judge. If you choose, the judge can approve your decree at a final hearing. A final hearing can be scheduled after the passing of the sixty-day or ninety-day mandatory waiting period under Tennessee law, assuming you and your spouse have also resolved all matters pertaining to your minor children.

If a property settlement agreement is reached by the parties, a court date for your final hearing can often be obtained earlier than a trial date, because a final hearing requires much less time than a trial. However, some jurisdictions allow entry of a final decree by affidavit. Ask your lawyer about the local rules in your judicial district.

11.38 If my spouse and I think our property settlement agreement is fair, why does the judge have to approve it?

The judge has a duty to ensure that all property settlement agreements in divorces are fair, reasonable, and equitable under Tennessee law. For this reason, your judge must review your agreement. The judge can consider the facts and circumstances of your case when reviewing the agreement. Not every case will result in an equal division of the assets and debts from the marriage, although this is very common.

11.39 What happens to the property distribution if one of us dies before the divorce proceedings are completed?

If your spouse dies prior to your divorce decree being entered, you will be considered married and treated as a surviving spouse under the law.

11.40 After our divorce is final, can the property agreement be modified?

Generally, provisions in your property settlement agreement or decree dealing with the distribution of your assets and debts are not modifiable. Absent an uncommon instance of fraud, duress, or newly discovered evidence, the property settlement agreement cannot be modified.

12

Benefits: Insurance, Retirement, and Pensions

During your marriage, you might have taken certain employment benefits for granted. You might not have given much thought each month to having insurance through your spouse's work. When you find yourself in a divorce, suddenly these benefits come to the forefront of your mind.

You might also, even unconsciously, have seen your own employment retirement benefits as belonging to you and not to your spouse and referred to "my 401(k)" or "my pension." After all, you are the one who went to work every day to earn it, right?

When you divorce, some benefits arising from your spouse's employment will end, some may continue for a period of time, and others may be divided between you. Retirement funds, in particular, are often one of the most valuable marital assets to be divided in a divorce.

Whether the benefits are from your employer or from your spouse's, with your attorney's help you will develop a better understanding of which benefits the law considers to be "yours" "mine," and "ours" for continuing or dividing.

12.1 Will my children continue to have health coverage through my spouse's work even though we're divorcing?

If either you or your spouse currently provides health insurance for your children, it is very likely that the court will order the insurance to remain in place until your child reaches the age of majority, or for so long as it remains available, and support is being paid for your child.

The cost of insurance for the children will be taken into consideration in determining the amount of child support to be paid.

12.2 Will I continue to have health insurance through my spouse's work after the divorce?

Generally, no. Investigate the cost of continuing on your spouse's employer-provided plans under a federal law known as *COBRA* after the expiration of your previous coverage. This coverage can be maintained for up to three years. However, the cost can be very high, so you will want to determine whether it's a realistic option.

Begin early to investigate your options for your future health insurance. The cost of your health care is an important factor when pursuing spousal support and planning your post-divorce budget.

12.3 What is a *qualified domestic relations order*?

A *qualified domestic relations order (QDRO)* is a court order that requires a retirement or pension plan administrator pay you the share of your former spouse's retirement that was awarded to you in the decree. These orders help ensure that a nonemployee spouse receives his or her share directly from the employee spouse's plan.

Obtaining a QDRO is a critical step in the divorce process. They can be complex documents, and a number of steps are required to reduce future concerns about enforcement and to fully protect your rights. These court orders must comply with numerous technical rules and be approved by the plan administrator, which is often located outside Tennessee.

Whenever possible, court orders dividing retirement plans should be entered at the same time as the decree of dissolution.

12.4 Must I have been married a certain number of years to be eligible to receive a part of my spouse's retirement fund or pension?

To be eligible to receive a part of your spouse's retirement or pension fund, some companies require that you be married for a certain length of time. However, even if your marriage is not of long duration, you may be entitled to a portion of your spouse's retirement fund or pension accumulated during the marriage. For example, if you were married for three years and your spouse contributed $10,000 to a 401(k) plan during the marriage, it is possible that the court would award you half of the value of the contribution when dividing your property and debts.

12.5 I contributed to my pension plan for ten years before I got married. Will my spouse get half of my entire pension?

Probably not. It is more likely the court will award your spouse only a portion of your retirement that was acquired during the marriage.

If either you or your spouse made premarital contributions to a pension or retirement plan, be sure to let your attorney know. This information is essential to determine which portion of the retirement plan should be treated as "premarital" and thus unlikely to be shared.

12.6 I plan to keep my same job after my divorce. Will my former spouse get half of the money I contribute to my retirement plan after my divorce?

No. Your former spouse should be entitled only to a portion of your retirement accumulated during the marriage.

Talk with your attorney so that the language of the court order ensures protection of your postdivorce retirement contributions.

12.7 Am I still entitled to a share of my spouse's retirement plan even though I never contributed to one of my own plans during our marriage?

Probably. Retirements are often the most valuable asset accumulated during a marriage. Consequently, your judge will consider the retirement along with all of the other marital assets and debts when determining a fair division.

12.8 How will I know the exact amount of my future monthly pension payment after the divorce?

More than one factor will determine your rights to collect from your spouse's retirement. One factor will be the terms of the court order dividing the retirement. The court order will tell you whether you are entitled to a set dollar amount, a percentage, or a fraction to be determined based upon the length of your marriage and how long your spouse continues working. For a defined benefit plan, such as a pension, the fraction used by the court to determine how much you are eligible to receive will be the number of years you were married while your spouse was employed at that company divided by the total number of years your spouse is employed with the company.

Another factor will be the terms of the retirement plan itself. Some provide for lump sum withdrawals; others issue payments in monthly installments. Review both the terms of your court order and contact the plan administrator to obtain the clearest understanding of your rights and benefits.

12.9 If I am eligible to receive my spouse's retirement benefits, when am I eligible to begin collecting it? Do I have to be sixty-five to collect it?

It depends upon the terms of your spouse's retirement plan. In some cases it is possible to begin receiving your share at the earliest date your spouse is eligible to receive them, regardless of whether he or she elects to do so. Check the terms of your spouse's plan to learn your options.

12.10 Am I entitled to cost-of-living increases on my share of my spouse's retirement?

It depends. If your spouse has a retirement plan that includes a provision for a *cost-of-living allowance (COLA)*, talk to your lawyer about whether this can be included in the court order dividing the retirement.

12.11 Does the death of my spouse affect the payout of retirement benefits to me or to our children?

It depends upon both the nature of your spouse's retirement plan and the terms of the court order dividing the retirement. If you want to be eligible for survivorship benefits from your spouse's pension, discuss the issue with your attorney before your case is settled or goes to trial.

Some plans allow only a surviving spouse or former spouse to be a beneficiary. Others may allow for the naming of an alternate beneficiary, such as your children.

12.12 Can I still collect on my former spouse's Social Security benefits if he or she passes on before I do?

It depends. You may be eligible to receive benefits if:

- You were married to your spouse for ten or more years.
- You are not remarried.
- You are at least sixty-two years old.
- The benefit you would receive based on your own earning record is less than the benefit you would receive from your former spouse.

For more information, contact your local Social Security Administration office or visit the SSA website at www.ssa.gov.

12.13 What orders might the court enter regarding life insurance?

The judge may order you or your spouse to maintain a life insurance policy to ensure that future support payments, such as child support and alimony, are made. In most cases you will be required to pay for your own life insurance after your divorce, and you should include this as an expense in your monthly budget.

12.14 Because we share children, should I consider my spouse as a beneficiary on my life insurance?

It depends upon your intentions. If your intention is to give the money to your former spouse, by all means name the other parent as beneficiary.

However, if you intend the life insurance proceeds to be used for the benefit of your children, talk with your attorney about your options. You may consider naming a trustee to manage the life insurance proceeds on behalf of your children, and there may be reasons to choose someone other than your former spouse.

12.15 Can the court require in the decree that I be the beneficiary of my spouse's insurance policy, so long as the children are minors or indefinitely?

When a court order is entered for life insurance, it is ordinarily for the purposes of ensuring payment of future support and will terminate when the support obligation has ended. Naming you as the beneficiary on your spouse's insurance policy for purposes of ensuring payment of future child support is one option. The court may also name the children directly as beneficiaries, or require a trust be established to receive the life insurance proceeds on behalf of your children.

12.16 My spouse is in the military. What are my rights to benefits after the divorce?

As the former spouse of a military member, the types of benefits to which you may be entitled are typically determined by the number of years you were married, the number of years your spouse was in the military while you were married, and whether or not you have remarried. Be sure you obtain accurate information about these dates.

Among the benefits for which you may be eligible are:

- A portion of your spouse's military retirement pay
- A survivor benefit in the event of your spouse's death
- Health care or participation in a temporary, transitional health care program
- Ability to keep your military identification card
- Use of certain military facilities, such as the commissary

Educate yourself about your right to future military benefits so that you can plan for your future with clarity. If your divorce is still pending, contact your base legal office or, for more information, visit the website for the branch of the military of which your spouse was a member.

13

Division of Debts

Throughout a marriage, most couples will have disagreements about money from time to time. You might think extra money should be spent on a family vacation, but your spouse might insist it should be saved for your retirement. You might think it's time to finally buy a new car, but your spouse thinks your driving the ten-year-old van for two more years is a better idea.

If you and your spouse had different philosophies about saving and spending during your marriage, chances are you will have some differing opinions when dividing your debts in divorce. What you both can count on is that Tennessee law provides that, to reach a fair outcome, the payment of debts must also be taken into consideration when dividing the assets from your marriage.

There are steps you can take to ensure the best outcome possible when it comes to dividing your marital debt. These include providing accurate and complete debt information to your lawyer and asking your lawyer to include provisions in your divorce decree to protect you in the future if your spouse refuses to pay his or her share.

Regardless of how the debts from your marriage are divided, know that you will gradually build your financial independence after your divorce is final.

13.1 Who is responsible for paying credit card bills and making house payments during the divorce proceedings?

In most cases, the court will not make decisions regarding the payment of credit card debt on a temporary basis. Work with your attorney and your spouse to reach a temporary agreement. Discuss the importance of making at least minimum payments on time to avoid substantial finance charges and late fees.

Typically, the spouse who remains in the home will be responsible for the mortgage payments, taxes, utilities, and most other ordinary expenses.

If you are concerned that you cannot afford to stay in the marital home on a temporary basis, talk with your attorney about your options prior to your temporary hearing.

13.2 What, if anything, should I be doing with the credit card companies as we go through the divorce?

If possible, it is best to obtain some separate credit prior to the divorce. This will help you establish credit in your own name and help you with necessary purchases following a separation.

Begin by obtaining a copy of your credit report from at least two of the three nationwide consumer reporting companies: Experian, Equifax, or TransUnion. The Fair Credit Reporting Act entitles you to a free copy of your credit report from each of these three companies every twelve months.

To order your free annual report online, go to www.annualcreditreport.com, call toll-free to (877) 322-8228, or complete an Annual Credit Report Request Form and mail it to: Annual Credit Report Request Service, P.O. Box 105281, Atlanta, Georgia 30348-5281. You can print the form from the Federal Trade Commission website at www.ftc.gov/credit.

Your spouse may have incurred debt using your name. This information is important to relay to your attorney. If you and your spouse have joint credit card accounts, contact each credit card company to close the account. Do the same if your spouse is an authorized user on any of your accounts.

If you want to maintain credit with a company, ask to have a new account in your own name. Be sure to let your spouse know if you close an account he or she has been using.

13.3   How is credit card debt divided?

Credit card debt will be divided as part of the overall division of the marital property and debts. Just as in the division of property, the court considers what is equitable, or fair, in your case.

If your spouse has exclusively used a credit card for purposes that did not benefit the family, such as gambling, talk with your attorney. In most cases the court will not review a lengthy history of how you and your spouse used the credit cards, but there can be exceptions.

13.4   Am I responsible for repayment of my spouse's student loans?

It depends. If your spouse incurred student loans prior to the marriage, it is most likely that he or she will be ordered to pay that debt.

If the debt was incurred during the marriage, how the funds were used may have an impact on who is ordered to pay them. For example, if your spouse borrowed $3,000 during the marriage for tuition, it is likely your spouse will be ordered to pay that debt. However, if a $3,000 student loan was taken out by your spouse, but $1,000 of it was used for a family vacation, then the court would be more likely to order the debt shared. The court may also consider payment on student loan debt when calculating the amount of child support to be paid.

If you were a joint borrower on your spouse's student loan and your spouse fails to pay the loan, the lender may attempt to collect from you even if your spouse has been ordered to pay the debt.

If either you or your spouse has student loan debt, be sure to give your attorney the complete history regarding the debt and ask about the most likely outcome under the facts of your case.

13.5 During the divorce proceedings, am I still responsible for debt my spouse continues to accrue?

It depends. In most cases the court will order each of the parties to be responsible for his or her own post-separation debts. In some cases, the date for dividing debt is when the parties separated households; in others, it is the date the complaint for divorce was filed.

13.6 During the marriage my spouse applied for and received several credit cards without my knowledge. Am I responsible for them?

It depends. The court will consider the overall fairness of the property and debt division when deciding who should pay this debt. If your spouse bought items with the cards and intends to keep those items, it is likely that she or he will be ordered to pay the debt incurred for the purchases.

13.7 During our marriage, we paid off thousands of dollars of debt incurred by my spouse before we were married. Will the court take this into consideration when dividing our property and debt?

It might. Just as premarital assets can have an impact on the overall division of property and debts, so can premarital debt. Depending upon the length of the marriage, the evidence of the debt, and the amount paid, it may be a factor for the judge to consider.

Be sure to let your attorney know if either you or your spouse brought substantial debt into the marriage.

13.8 Regarding debts, what is a *hold-harmless provision*, and why should it be in the divorce decree?

A *hold-harmless provision* is intended to protect you in the event that your spouse fails to follow a court order to pay a debt after the divorce is granted. The language typically provides that your spouse shall "indemnify and hold [you] harmless from liability" on the debt.

If you and your spouse have a joint debt and your spouse fails to pay, the creditor may nevertheless attempt to collect from you. This is because the court is without power to change the creditor's rights and can make orders affecting only you and your spouse.

In the event your spouse fails to pay a court-ordered debt and the creditor attempts collection from you, the hold-harmless provision in your divorce decree can be used in an effort to insist that payment is made by your former spouse.

13.9 My spouse and I have agreed that I will keep our home; why must I refinance the mortgage?

There may be a number of reasons why your spouse is asking you to refinance the mortgage. First, the mortgage company cannot be forced to take your spouse's name off of the mortgage note. This means that if you did not make the house payments, the lender could pursue collection against your spouse.

Second, your spouse may want to receive his or her share of the home equity. It may be possible for you to borrow additional money at the time of refinancing to pay your spouse his or her share of the equity in the home.

Third, the mortgage on your family home may prevent your spouse from buying a home in the future. Because there remains a risk that your spouse could be pursued for the debt to the mortgage company, it is unlikely that a second lender will want to take the risk of extending further credit to your spouse.

13.10 Can I file for bankruptcy while my divorce is pending?

Yes. Consult with your attorney if you are considering filing for bankruptcy while your divorce is pending. It will be important for you to ask questions such as:

- Should I file for bankruptcy on my own or with my spouse?
- How will filing for bankruptcy affect my ability to purchase a home in the future?
- Which debts can be discharged in bankruptcy and which cannot?
- How will a bankruptcy affect the division of property and debts in the divorce?

- How might a delay in the divorce proceeding due to a bankruptcy impact my case?
- What form of bankruptcy is best for my situation?

If you use a different attorney for your bankruptcy than for your divorce, be sure each attorney is kept fully informed about the developments in the other case.

13.11 What happens if my spouse files for bankruptcy during our divorce?

Contact your attorney right away. The filing of a bankruptcy while your divorce is pending can have a significant impact on your divorce. Your attorney can advise you whether certain debts are likely to be discharged in the bankruptcy, the delay a bankruptcy may cause to your divorce, and whether bankruptcy is an appropriate option for you.

13.12 Can I file for divorce while I am in bankruptcy?

Yes, however, you must receive the bankruptcy court's permission to proceed with the divorce. In bankruptcy, your property is protected from debt collection by the *automatic stay*. The stay can also prevent the divorce court from dividing property between you and your spouse until you obtain the bankruptcy court's permission to proceed with the divorce.

13.13 What should I do if my former spouse files for bankruptcy after our divorce?

Contact your attorney immediately. If you learn that your former spouse has filed for bankruptcy, you may have certain rights to object to the discharge of any debts your spouse was ordered to pay under your divorce decree. If you fail to take action, it is possible that you will be held responsible for debts your spouse was ordered to pay.

13.14 If I am awarded child support or alimony in my decree, can these obligations be discharged if my former spouse files for bankruptcy after our divorce?

No, support obligations such as child support and alimony are not dischargeable in bankruptcy, meaning these debts cannot be eliminated in a bankruptcy proceeding.

13.15 What happens if my former spouse does not pay their obligations in the decree?

If your former spouse does not pay the debts assigned to him or her in the decree, you may be able to pursue a contempt of court action. A party is in contempt of court if they willfully disobey or disregard a court order. Talk with your attorney to determine whether a contempt of court action may be filed in your case to enforce your rights under your decree.

14

Taxes

Nobody likes a surprise letter from the Internal Revenue Service saying he or she owes more taxes. When your divorce is over, you want to be sure you don't later discover you owe taxes you weren't expecting to pay.

A number of tax issues may arise during your divorce. Your attorney may not be able to answer all of your tax questions, so you may need to consult with an accountant or tax advisor for additional advice.

Taxes are important considerations in both settlement negotiations and trial preparation. They should not be overlooked. Taxes can impact many of your decisions, including those regarding spousal maintenance, division of property, and the receipt of benefits. Be sure to ask the professionals helping you about the tax implications in your divorce so you don't get that letter in the mail that begins, "Dear Taxpayer:..."

14.1 Will either my spouse or I have to pay income tax when we transfer property or pay a property settlement to one another according to our divorce decree?

No. However, it is important that you see the future tax consequences of a subsequent withdrawal, sale, or transfer of certain assets you receive in your divorce.

It is important to ask your attorney to take tax consequences into consideration when looking at the division of your assets.

14.2   Is the amount of child support I pay tax deductible?
No.

14.3   Do I have to pay income tax on any child support I receive?
No. Your child support is tax free, regardless of when it is paid or when it is received.

14.4   What does the IRS consider alimony?
Amounts paid under a divorce decree or according to a written separation agreement entered into between you and your spouse will be considered alimony if:

- You and your spouse or former spouse do not file a joint return with each other.
- The payment is in cash, check, or money orders.
- The payment is received by (or on behalf of) your spouse or former spouse.

Not all payments made according to a divorce or separation decree are alimony. Alimony does not include:

- Child support
- Noncash property settlements
- Payments to keep up the payer's property
- Use of the payor's property

14.5   Is the amount of alimony I am ordered to pay tax deductible?
Most of the time. Spousal support paid pursuant to a court order is usually deductible. This will include court-ordered alimony and may also include other forms of support provided to your former spouse (but not child support). Your tax deduction is a factor to consider when determining a fair amount of alimony to be paid in your case. Alimony may not be taxable if it is non-modifiable according to the terms of the final decree. This is also referred to as *alimony in solido.*

14.6   Do I have to pay tax on the alimony that I receive?

Most of the time. With the exception of alimony *in solido*, you must pay income tax on the spousal support you receive. This will include court-ordered alimony and may also include other forms of spousal support, but not child support, paid by your spouse.

Income tax is a critical factor in determining a fair amount of alimony. Taxes must be considered when looking at your monthly living expenses for the purposes of seeking an alimony award. Insist that your attorney bring this issue to the attention of your spouse's lawyer, or to the judge, if your case proceeds to trial, so that both the tax you pay and the deduction your spouse receives are taken into consideration.

It is important to budget for payment of tax on your alimony. Be sure to consult with your tax advisor. Making estimated tax payments throughout the year or withholding additional taxes from your wages can avoid a burdensome tax liability at the end of the year.

14.7   During the divorce proceedings, is our tax filing status affected?

It can be. You are considered unmarried if your decree is final by December 31 of the tax year.

If you are considered unmarried, your filing status is either "single" or, under certain circumstances, "head of household." If your decree is not final as of December 31, your filing status is either "married filing a joint return" or "married filing a separate return," unless you live apart from your spouse and meet the exception for "head of household."

While your divorce is in progress, talk to both your tax advisor and your attorney about your filing status. It may be beneficial to figure your tax on both a joint return and a separate return to see which gives you the lower tax. IRS Publication 504, Divorced or Separated Individuals, provides more detail on tax issues while you are going through a divorce.

14.8 Should I file a joint income tax return with my spouse while our divorce is pending?

Consult your tax advisor to determine the risks and benefits of filing a joint return with your spouse. Compare this with the consequences of filing your tax return separately. Often, the overall tax liability will be less with the filing of a joint return, but other factors are important to consider.

When deciding whether to file a joint return with your spouse, consider any concerns you have about the accuracy and truthfulness of the information on the tax return. If you have any doubts, consult both your attorney and your tax advisor before agreeing to sign a joint tax return with your spouse. Prior to filing a return with your spouse, try to reach agreement about how any tax owed or refund expected will be shared, and ask your lawyer to assist you in getting this in writing.

14.9 My spouse will not cooperate in providing the necessary documents to prepare or file our taxes jointly. What options do I have?

Talk with your attorney about requesting your spouse to cooperate in the preparation and filing of your joint return. If your spouse persists in his or her refusal to cooperate, your attorney may seek court intervention.

14.10 For tax purposes, is one time of year better to divorce than another?

It depends upon your tax situation. If you and your spouse agree that it would be beneficial to file joint tax returns for the year in which you are divorcing, you may wish to not have your divorce finalized before the end of the year.

Your marital status for filing income taxes is determined by your status on December 31. Consequently, if you both want to preserve your right to file a joint return, your decree should not be entered before December 1 of that year.

14.11 What tax consequences should I consider regarding the sale of our home?

When your home is sold, whether during your divorce or after, the sale may be subject to a capital gains tax. If your home was your primary residence and you lived in the home for two of the preceding five years, you may be eligible to exclude up to $250,000 of the gain on the sale of your home. If both you and your spouse meet the ownership and residence requirements, you may be eligible to exclude up to $500,000 of the gain.

If you anticipate the gain on the sale of your residence to be over $250,000, talk with your attorney early in the divorce process about a plan to minimize the tax liability. For more information, see IRS Publication 523, Selling Your Home, or visit the IRS website at www.irs.gov and talk with your tax advisor.

14.12 How might capital gains tax be a problem for me years after the divorce?

Future capital gains tax on the sale of property should be discussed with your attorney during the negotiation and trial preparation stages of your case. This is especially important if the sale of the property is imminent. Failure to do so may result in an unfair outcome.

For example, suppose you agree that your spouse will be awarded the proceeds from the sale of your home valued at $200,000, after the real estate commission, and you will take the stock portfolio also valued at $200,000.

Suppose that after the divorce you decide to sell the stock. It is still valued at $200,000, but you learn that its original price was $120,000 and that you must pay capital gains tax of 15 percent on the $80,000 of gain. You pay tax of $12,000, leaving you with $188,000.

Meanwhile, your former spouse sells the marital home but pays no capital gains tax because he qualifies for the $250,000 exemption. (*See* question 14.11 above.) He is left with the full $200,000.

Tax implications of your property division should always be discussed with your attorney, with support from your tax advisor as needed.

14.13 During and after the divorce, who gets to claim the children as dependents?

This issue should be addressed in settlement negotiations or at trial, if settlement is not reached.

The judge has discretion to determine which parent will be entitled to claim the children as exemptions for income tax purposes. Where child support has been ordered pursuant to the Tennessee Child Support Guidelines, many judges order that the exemptions be shared or alternated. However, most judges will order that the payor of child support be current on his or her child-support obligation to be eligible to claim the income tax dependency exemption. Additionally, if one party has income so low or so high that he or she will not benefit from the dependency exemption, the court may award the exemption to the other parent.

14.14 My decree says I have to sign IRS Form 8332 so my former spouse can claim our child as an exemption, since I have custody. Should I sign it once for all future years?

No. Child custody and child support can be modified in the future. If there is a future modification of custody or support, which parent is entitled to claim your child as an exemption could change. The best practice is to provide your former spouse a timely copy of Form 8332 signed by you for the appropriate tax year only.

14.15 Do I have to pay taxes on the portion of my spouse's 401(k) that was awarded to me in the divorce?

If you have been awarded a portion of your former spouse's 401(k) or 403(b) retirement plan, any distribution of these funds to you will be subject to regular income tax. However, it may be possible for you to elect to receive all or a portion of these assets without incurring the 10 percent early-withdrawal penalty (applicable if you are under age fifty-nine and one half) if you decide to take the money rather than keeping an account in your name or rolling over the assets to an IRA or other permitted retirement account. Talk with your attorney and your tax advisor to determine your options.

14.16 Is the cost of getting a divorce, including my attorney fees, tax deductible under any circumstances?

Your legal fees for getting a divorce are not deductible. However, a portion of your attorney fees may be deductible if they are for:

- The collection of sums included in your gross income, such as alimony or interest income

- Advice regarding the determination of taxes or tax due

Attorney fees are "miscellaneous" deductions for individuals and are consequently limited to 2 percent of your adjusted gross income. More details can be found in IRS Publication 529, Miscellaneous Deductions.

You may also be able to deduct fees you pay to appraisers or accountants who help. Talk to your tax advisor about whether any portion of your attorney fees or other expenses from your divorce is deductible.

14.17 Do I have to complete a new Form W-4 for my employer because of my divorce?

Completing a new Form W-4, Employee's Withholding Certificate, will help you to claim the proper withholding allowances based upon your marital status and exemptions. Also, if you receive alimony, you may need to make arrangements for the tax due on the alimony income. Consult with your tax advisor to ensure you are making the most preferable tax-planning decision.

14.18 What is *innocent spouse relief* and how can it help me?

Innocent spouse relief refers to a method of obtaining relief from the Internal Revenue Service for taxes you owe if your spouse or former spouse failed to report income, reported income improperly, or claimed improper deductions or credits on a joint income tax return filed during your marriage.

Numerous factors affect your eligibility for innocent spouse tax relief, such as:

- You would suffer a financial hardship if you were required to pay the tax.

- You did not significantly benefit from the unpaid taxes.

Taxes

- You suffered abuse during your marriage.
- You thought your spouse would pay the taxes on the original return.

Talk with your attorney or tax advisor if you are concerned about liability for taxes arising from joint tax returns filed during the marriage. You may benefit from a referral to an attorney who specializes in tax law.

15

Going to Court

For many of us, our images of going to court are created by movies and our favorite television shows. We picture the witness breaking down in tears after a grueling cross-examination. We see lawyers strutting around the courtroom, waving their arms as they plead their case to the jury.

Hollywood drama, however, is a far cry from reality. Going to court for your divorce can mean many things, ranging from sitting in a hallway while waiting for the lawyers and judges to conclude a conference, to being on the witness stand giving mundane answers to questions about your monthly living expenses.

Regardless of the nature of your court proceeding, going to court often evokes a sense of anxiety. Perhaps your divorce might be the first time in your life that you have even been in a courtroom. Be assured that these feelings of nervousness and uncertainty are normal.

Understanding what will occur in court and being well prepared for any court hearings will relieve much of your stress. Knowing the order of events, courtroom etiquette, the role of the people in the courtroom, and what is expected of you will make the entire experience easier.

Your lawyer will be with you at all times to support you any time you go to court. Remember, every court appearance moves you one step closer to completing your divorce so that you can move forward with your life.

Going to Court

15.1 What do I need to know about appearing in court and court dates in general?

Court dates are important. As soon as you receive a notice from your attorney about a court date in your case, confirm whether your attendance will be required and put the date on your calendar.

Ask your attorney about the nature of the hearing, including whether the judge will be listening to testimony by witnesses, reading affidavits, or merely listening to the arguments of the lawyers.

Ask whether it is necessary for you to meet with your attorney or take any other action to prepare for the hearing, such as providing additional information or documents.

Find out how long the hearing is expected to last. It may be as short as a few minutes or as long as a day or more.

If you plan to attend the hearing, determine where and when to meet your attorney. Depending upon the type of hearing, your lawyer may want you to arrive in advance of the scheduled hearing time to prepare.

Make sure you know the location of the courthouse, where to park, and the floor and room number of the courtroom. Planning for such simple matters as having change available for a parking meter can eliminate unnecessary stress. If you want someone to go to court with you to provide you support, check with your attorney first.

15.2 When and how often will I need to go to court?

Whether and how often you will need to go to court depend upon a number of factors. Depending upon the complexity of your case, you may have only one hearing or numerous court hearings throughout the course of your divorce.

Some hearings, usually those on procedural matters, are attended only by the attorneys. These could include requests for the other side to provide information or for the setting of certain deadlines. These hearings are often brief and held in the judge's chambers rather than in the courtroom. Other hearings, such as temporary hearings for custody or support, are typically attended by both parties and their attorneys.

If you and your spouse settle all of the issues in your case, although not required, you can choose to testify at a

179

final hearing in which the judge will review and approve your decree.

If your case proceeds to trial, your appearance will be required for the duration of the trial. In Tennessee, divorce matters are almost always heard before a judge only; juries very rarely hear divorces.

15.3 How much notice will I receive about appearing in court?

The amount of notice you will receive for any court hearing can vary from a few days to several weeks. Ask your attorney whether and when it will be necessary for you to appear in court on your case so that you can have time to prepare and plan.

If you receive a notice of a hearing, contact your attorney immediately. He or she can tell you whether your appearance is required and what other steps are needed to prepare.

15.4 I am afraid to be alone in the same room with my spouse. When I go to court, is this going to happen if the attorneys go into the judge's chambers to discuss the case?

Talk to your lawyer. Prior to any court hearing, you and your spouse may be asked to wait while your attorneys meet with the judge to discuss preliminary matters.

A number of options are likely to be available to ensure that you feel safe. These might include having you and your spouse wait in different locations or having a friend or family member present.

Your lawyer wants to support you in feeling secure throughout all court proceedings. Just let him or her know your concerns.

15.5 Do I have to go to court every time there is a court hearing on any motion?

Not necessarily. Some matters will be decided by the judge after listening to the arguments of the lawyers. These hearings are usually held in the judge's office, referred to as "chambers," and you will not be required to attend.

15.6 My spouse's attorney keeps asking for continuances of court dates. Is there anything I can do to stop this?

Continuances of court dates are not unusual in divorces. A court date might be postponed for many reasons, including a conflict on the calendar of one of the attorneys or the judge, the lack of availability of one of the parties or an important witness, or the need for more time to prepare.

Discuss with your attorney your desire to move your case forward without further delay, so that repeated requests for continuances can be resisted.

15.7 If I have to go to court, will I be put on the stand? Will there be a jury?

In Tennessee, divorce matters are almost always heard before a judge only; juries almost never hear divorces. Whether you will be put on the stand will depend upon the nature of the issues in dispute, the judge assigned to your case, and your attorney's strategy for your case.

15.8 My attorney said I need to be in court for our *temporary hearing* next week. What's going to happen?

A *temporary hearing* is held to determine such matters as who remains in the house while your divorce is pending, temporary custody, temporary support, and other financial matters.

The procedure for your temporary hearing can vary depending upon the county in which your case was filed, the judge to which the case is assigned, and whether temporary custody is disputed.

Most temporary hearings are held on the basis of written affidavits and the arguments of the lawyers. While you should plan to attend your temporary hearing, it is possible that the hearing will be held in the judge's chambers with only the judge and attorneys present.

Even if your temporary hearing is held in the judge's chambers, your presence at the hearing is still important. Your attorney may need additional information from you during the hearing, and last-minute negotiations to resolve temporary issues are not uncommon.

In some counties, your hearing will be one of numerous other hearings on the judge's calendar. You may find yourself in a courtroom with many other lawyers and their clients, all having matters scheduled before the court that day. Even though you are present in the courtroom, your attorney will make your argument to the judge and it is unlikely you will be required to provide formal testimony.

If temporary custody is disputed, you and other witnesses might be required to take the witness stand to give testimony at your temporary hearing. If this is the case, meeting with your attorney in advance to fully prepare is very important.

Talk to your lawyer about the procedure you should expect for the temporary hearing in your case.

15.9 Are there any rules about courtroom etiquette that I need to know?

Knowing a few tips about being in the courtroom will make your experience easier.

- Dress appropriately. Avoid overly casual dress, a lot of jewelry, revealing clothing, and extreme hairstyles.
- Do not bring beverages into the courtroom. Most courts have rules that do not allow food and drink in courtrooms. If you need water, ask your attorney.
- Dispose of chewing gum before entering the court.
- Do not talk aloud in the courtroom unless you are on the witness stand, being questioned by the judge.
- Do not enter the judge's office.
- Stand up whenever the judge is entering or leaving the courtroom.
- Be sure to turn off your electronic devices.
- Be mindful that the judge may be observing you during the hearing and a negative image may hurt your result.

15.10 What is the role of the *court officer*?

The *court officer* provides support for the judge and lawyers in the management of the court calendar and the courtroom. He or she assists in the scheduling of court hearings and the management of legal documents given to the judge for review, such as temporary orders and divorce decrees.

15.11 Will there be a *court reporter,* and what will he or she do?

A *court reporter* is a professional trained to make an accurate record of the words spoken and documents offered into evidence during court proceedings.

A written transcript of a court proceeding may be purchased from the court reporter. If your case is appealed, the transcript prepared by the court reporter will be used by the appeals court to review the facts of your case.

The court reporter is also responsible for managing documents and other items offered into evidence at trial.

Some hearings are held "off the record," which means that the court reporter is not making a record of what is being said. Ordinarily, these are matters for which no appeal is expected to be taken.

15.12 Will I be able to talk to my attorney while we are in court?

During court proceedings it is important that your attorney give his or her full attention to anything being said by the judge, witnesses, or your spouse's lawyer. For this reason, your attorney will avoid talking with you when anyone else in the courtroom is speaking.

Plan to have pen and paper with you when you go to court. If your court proceeding is underway and your lawyer is listening to what is being said by others in the courtroom, write him or her a note with your questions or comments.

It is critical that your attorney hear each question asked by the other lawyer and all answers given by each witness. If not, opportunities for making objections to inappropriate evidence may be lost. You can support your attorney in doing an effective job for you by avoiding talking to him or her while a court hearing is in progress.

If your court hearing is lengthy, breaks will be taken. You can use this time to discuss with your attorney any questions or observations you have about the proceeding.

15.13 My attorney said the judge has issued a *pretrial order* and I must comply with it. What does this mean?

Some judges will order certain information be provided either to the opposing party or to the judge in advance of trial. This is called a *pretrial order*. This might include:

- A list of issues that have been settled
- A list of issues that are still disputed
- Agreements, referred to as *stipulations,* as to the truth of certain facts
- The names of witnesses
- Exhibits
- A summary of how you want the judge to decide the case
- Deadlines for providing information.

Ask your attorney for a copy of the pretrial order.

15.14 What is a *pretrial conference*?

A *pretrial conference* is a meeting held with the attorneys and the judge to review information related to an upcoming trial, such as:

- How long the trial is expected to last
- The issues in dispute
- The law surrounding the disputed issues
- The identification of witnesses
- The identification of trial exhibits
- The status of negotiations

Often, the trial date is set at the pretrial conference. If a pretrial conference is held in your case, ask your attorney whether you should attend. Your attorney may request that you either be present for the conference or be available by phone.

15.15 Besides meeting with my attorney, is there anything else I should do to prepare for my upcoming trial?

Yes. Be sure to review your deposition and any information you provided in your discovery, such as answers to interrogatories. Also be sure to review any affidavits previously submitted to the judge, such as your financial or child support affidavit prepared for your temporary hearing. It is possible that you will be asked some of the same questions at trial. If you think you might give different answers at trial, discuss this with your lawyer.

It is important that your attorney know in advance of trial whether any information you provided during the discovery process has changed.

15.16 I'm meeting with my attorney to prepare for trial. How do I make the most of this meeting?

Meeting with your attorney to prepare for your trial is important to achieving a good outcome. Come to the meeting prepared to discuss the following:

- The issues in your case
- Your desired outcome on each of the issues
- The questions you might be asked at trial by both attorneys
- The exhibits that will be offered into evidence during the trial
- The witnesses for your trial
- The status of negotiations

Meeting with your attorney will help you to better understand what to expect at trial and make the trial experience easier.

15.17 How do I know who my witnesses will be at trial?

Well in advance of your trial date, your lawyer will discuss with you whether other witnesses, besides you and your spouse, will be necessary. Witnesses can include family members, friends, child-care providers, clergy members, etc. When thinking of potential witnesses, consider your relationship with the witness, whether that witness has had an opportunity to observe relevant facts, and whether the witness has knowledge different from that of other witnesses.

You may also have expert witnesses testify on your behalf. An expert witness will provide opinion testimony based upon specialized knowledge, training, or experience. For example, a psychologist, real estate appraiser, or accountant may provide expert testimony on your behalf.

15.18 My divorce is scheduled for trial. Does this mean there is no hope for a settlement?

Many cases are settled after a trial date is set. The setting of a trial date may cause you and your spouse to think about the risks and costs of going to trial. This can help you and your spouse focus on what is most important to you and lead you toward a negotiated settlement. Because the costs of preparing for and proceeding to trial are substantial, it is best to engage in settlement negotiations well in advance of your trial date. However, it is not uncommon for cases to settle a few days before trial, or even at the courthouse before your trial begins.

15.19 Can I prevent my spouse from being in the courtroom?

Probably not. Because your spouse has a legal interest in the outcome of your divorce, he or she has a right to be present. Tennessee courtrooms are open to the public. Consequently, it is not uncommon for persons not involved in your divorce to pass through the courtroom at various times simply because they have other business with the court.

15.20 Can I take a friend or family member with me to court?

Yes. Let your attorney know in advance if you intend to bring anyone to court with you. Some people important to you may be very emotional about your divorce or your spouse. Be sure to invite someone who is better able to focus attention on supporting you rather than on his or her own feelings.

15.21 Can my friends and family be present in the courtroom during my trial?

It depends upon whether they will be witnesses in your case. In most cases where witnesses other than the husband and wife are testifying, the attorneys request that the court sequester the witnesses. The judge would then order all witnesses, except you and your spouse, to leave the courtroom until after they have testified.

Once a witness has completed his or her testimony, he or she will ordinarily be allowed to remain in the courtroom for the remainder of the trial.

15.22 I want to do a great job testifying as a witness in my divorce trial. What are some tips?

Keep the following in mind to be a good witness on your own behalf:

- Listen carefully to the complete question before thinking of your answer.

- If you don't understand a question or don't know the answer, be sure to say so.

- Take your time. You may be asked questions that call for a thoughtful response. If you need a moment to reflect on an answer before you give it, allow yourself such time.

- Slow down. It is easy to speed up our speech when anxious. Taking your time with your answers ensures that the judge hears you and the court reporter can accurately record your testimony.

- Tell the truth. Although this may not be always be comfortable, it is critical if you want the judge to believe your testimony.

- If the question calls for a "yes" or "no" answer, simply say so. Then wait for the attorney to ask you the next question. If there is more you want to explain, remember that you have already told your attorney all the important facts and he or she will make sure you are allowed to give any testimony significant to your case.

- Do not argue with the judge or the attorneys.

- Stop speaking if an objection is made by one of the attorneys. Wait until the judge has instructed you to answer.

- If you begin to feel emotional, your attorney can ask for a short break.

15.23 Should I be worried about being cross-examined by my spouse's lawyer at trial?

If your case goes to trial, prepare to be asked some questions by your spouse's lawyer. Many of these questions will call for a simple "yes" or "no."

If you are worried about particular questions, discuss your concerns with your attorney. He or she can support you in giving a truthful response. Focus on preparing well for being asked questions by your spouse's lawyer. Try not to take the questions personally; remember that the lawyer is fulfilling a duty to advocate for your spouse's interests. Remember that you are just doing your best to tell the truth about the facts.

15.24 What happens on the day of trial?

Although no two trials are alike, the following steps will occur in most divorce trials:

- Attorneys meet with the judge in chambers to discuss procedural issues, such as how many witnesses will be called, how long the case will take to present, and when breaks might be taken.

- Attorneys give opening statements.

- Plaintiff's attorney calls plaintiff's witnesses to testify.

- Defendant's attorney may cross-examine each of them.

- Defendant's attorney calls defendant's witness to testify.

- Plaintiff's attorney may cross-examine each of them.

- Plaintiff's lawyer calls any rebuttal witnesses, that is, witnesses whose testimony contradicts the testimony of the defendant's witnesses.

- Closing arguments are made first by the plaintiff's attorney and then by the defendant's attorney.

15.25   Will the judge decide my case the day I go to court?

Possibly. Often, there is so much information from the trial for the judge to consider that it is not possible for the judge to give an immediate ruling.

The judge may want to review documents, review the law, perform calculations, review his or her notes, and give thoughtful consideration to the issues to be decided. For this reason, it may be days, weeks, or in some cases, even longer before a ruling is made.

When a judge does not make a ruling immediately upon the conclusion of a trial, it is said that the case has been "taken under advisement."

16

The Appeals Process

You may find that, despite your best efforts to settle your case, your divorce went to trial and the judge made major decisions that will have a serious impact on your future. You may be gravely disappointed or even shocked by the judge's ruling.

The judge might have seen your case differently than you and your attorney did. Perhaps the judge made mistakes. Or it may be that Tennessee law simply does not allow for the outcome you were hoping for.

Whatever the reasons for the court's rulings, you may feel that the judge's decisions are not ones that you can live with. If this is the case, talk to your lawyer immediately about your right to appeal. Together you can decide whether an appeal is in your best interests, or whether it is better to accept the court's ruling and invest your energy in moving forward with your life without an appeal.

16.1 How much time after my divorce do I have to file an appeal?

You must file an appeal within thirty days of the final order you wish to appeal. Because your attorney may also recommend filing certain motions following your trial, discuss your appeal rights with your lawyer as soon as you have received the judge's ruling.

A timely discussion with your attorney about your right to appeal is essential so important deadlines are not missed.

16.2   Can I appeal a temporary order?

Generally, no. Under Tennessee law, only final orders may be appealed except in very limited circumstances.

16.3   What parts of the decree can be appealed?

If you or your spouse is unhappy with final decisions made by the judge in your case, either of you can file an appeal. Decisions that can be appealed include custody, parenting time, child support, alimony, division of property, and attorney's fees.

16.4   Will my attorney recommend I appeal specific aspects of the decree, or will I have to request it?

Your attorney may counsel you to file an appeal on certain issues of your case; you may also ask your lawyer whether there is a legitimate basis for an appeal of any decision you believe is wrong. Talk to your attorney regarding the decisions most dissatisfying to you. Your lawyer can advise which issues have the greatest likelihood of success on appeal, in light of the facts of your case and Tennessee law.

16.5   When should an appeal be filed?

An appeal should only be filed when, after careful consultation with your attorney, you believe that the judge has made a serious error under the law or the facts of your case. Among the factors you should discuss with your attorney are:

*   Whether the judge had the authority under the law to make the decisions set forth in your decree
*   The likelihood of the success of your appeal
*   The risk that an appeal by you will encourage an appeal by your former spouse
*   The cost of the appeal
*   The length of time an appeal can be expected to take
*   The impact of a delay in the case during the appeal

The deadline for filing an appeal is thirty days from the date that a final order is entered in your case. It is important that you are clear about the deadline that applies in your case, so talk to your attorney at once if you are thinking about an appeal.

16.6   Are there any disadvantages to filing an appeal?

There can be disadvantages to filing an appeal, including:

- Uncertainty as to the outcome
- Increased attorney's fees and costs
- The risk of a worse outcome on appeal than you received at trial
- Delay of final resolution
- Prolonged conflict between you and your former spouse
- Risk of a second trial occurring after the appeal
- Difficulty in obtaining closure and moving forward with your life

16.7   Is it necessary to have an attorney in order to appeal?

The appeals process is very detailed and specific, with set deadlines and specific court rules. Given the complex nature of the appellate process, you should have an attorney if you intend to file an appeal.

16.8   How long does the appeals process usually take?

It depends. An appeal can take anywhere from several months to well over a year. An appeal may also result in the appellate court requiring further proceedings by the trial court. This will result in further delay.

16.9   What are the steps in the appeals process?

There are many steps your attorney will take on your behalf in the appeal process, including:

- Identifying the issues to be appealed
- Filing a notice with the court of your intent to appeal
- Obtaining the necessary court documents and trial exhibits to send to the appellate court
- Obtaining the trial transcript, a written copy of testimony by witnesses and statements by the judge and the lawyers made in the presence of the court reporter
- Performing legal research to support your arguments on appeal

- Preparing and filing a document known as a *brief,* which sets forth the facts of the case and relevant law, complete with citations to court transcript, court documents, and prior cases

- Making an oral argument before the judges of the appellate court

16.10   Is filing and pursuing an appeal expensive?

Yes. In addition to filing fees and attorney fees, there is likely to be a substantial cost for the preparation of the transcript of the trial testimony.

16.11   If I do not file an appeal, can I ever go back to court to change my decree?

Certain aspects of a decree are not modifiable, such as the division of property and debts or the award of attorney fees. Other parts of your decree, such as support or matters regarding the children, may be modified if there has been a "material and substantial change in circumstances."

A modification of custody or parenting time for minor children will also require you to show that the change would be in their best interests.

If your decree did not provide for alimony or if it ordered that the alimony be non-modifiable, it is unlikely that you will have any basis for a modification. If you believe that you have a basis for a modification of your divorce decree, consult with your attorney.

17

What Happens after the Divorce?

You have finally reached the end of the divorce journey. You may be feeling sad about the end of your marriage, you may be feeling hopeful about the future ahead of you, and you may be feeling scared about your new life coming to fruition. These feelings are normal.

It is also normal for you to feel uneasy that your lawyer is closing your file and you will be without him or her to support you through the days ahead. You may be feeling overwhelmed and unsure about how you take the final actions to complete property transfers or name-change details.

Whatever items are on your to-do list, it is best to map out your action plan. Clarify which items are your responsibility and, as with everything through this divorce process, start small.

17.1 What do I need to do when the amount of child support changes based on one of my children turning eighteen?

You should contact the child support attorney's office through the district attorney's office in your judicial district.

17.2 Do I need to inform the court if my employment changes?

If you pay support pursuant to your decree and you change employers, it will be necessary for you to complete a new Notice to Withhold Income form for your new employer.

You should do this as soon as possible to ensure child support is paid timely and to avoid an arrearage and interest charges.

17.3 **My decree includes a provision that my former spouse and I both pay a portion of uninsured medical expenses, child-care expenses, and other expenses incurred for the minor children. How do I track this information and when do I get reimbursed?**

Be sure to provide your former spouse with the appropriate documentation as set forth in your decree. Failure to request reimbursement of these expenses in a timely manner may result in your being barred from collecting them. Be sure to keep a copy of all documents you send to the other parent.

Reimbursement of uninsured medical expenses, as well as child-care or other related expenses, is an issue frequently disputed in modification and contempt of court matters. For this reason, maintain complete records regarding these expenses, such as:

- Keeping copies of all billing statements from the service providers with your notations regarding payments made to include the date, amount, and check number
- Keeping copies of all insurance benefits statements
- Asking your pharmacy to give you a monthly or an annual printout of all the charges and payments for prescription drugs
- Asking your child-care provider to give you a monthly or annual printout of all the charges and payments
- Keeping copies of any correspondence between you and the other parent regarding these expenses
- Keeping a record of sums paid by the other parent, either directly to care providers or reimbursements paid to you

Keep these records organized by year and/or by child. You may want to consider creating a work sheet to help you track expenses and payments. In the event of a future dispute, you will then have all of the documentation needed for your attorney to present your case or to defend a claim against you.

17.4 What if my former spouse and I have a disagreement about our parenting plan after the decree is entered?

Tennessee law provides that most future disputes are to be mediated prior to either party filing a new court action. If you have an unresolved parenting dispute, you should ask your attorney to begin the process of mediation.

17.5 My former spouse has not paid me the property settlement as ordered in the decree, what can I do?

In the event that your former spouse does not pay court-ordered judgments, enforcement mechanisms may be available, such as contempt of court actions or garnishment. If payment becomes a problem, contact your attorney to discuss your enforcement possibilities.

17.6 After my decree was entered, my former spouse did not pay a judgment and I did not do anything about it. Is it too late?

Judgments for property settlement and/or attorney fees are valid for ten years. If a judgment owed to you is not paid, in order to keep the judgment valid see your attorney about pursuing an extension and enforcement before the judgment lapses.

17.7 I restored my former name under my divorce decree, what do I need to do?

The following name-change checklist includes a list of people and places that you may want to contact to let them know your new name.

Name-Change Checklist

_____Banks and other financial institutions

_____Financial planner

_____Creditors (mortgage company, auto loan companies, credit cards)

_____Credit reporting agencies

_____Department of Motor Vehicles for auto registration

_____Driver's license

_____Department of Records and Vital Statistics

Name-Change Checklist   Continued

_____Deeds and property titles

_____Stock certificates

_____Employers

_____Friends and family

_____Insurance agencies (homeowner, car, health, life, annuities)

_____Passport office

_____Post office

_____Public assistance office

_____Registrar of voters

_____Schools (yours and your children's)

_____School alumni organizations

_____Social Security Administration (SSA)

_____Taxing authorities (city, state, federal)

_____Utility services (telephone, gas, electric, water, garbage)

_____Tennessee Child Support Receiving Unit

_____Internal Revenue Service (IRS)

_____Church/religious organizations

_____Frequently used service providers (stylist, lawn service)

_____Magazine/newspaper/publication subscriptions

_____Professional organizations

17.8 I was told by my bank that I need a certified copy of my decree. How do I obtain one?

Your decree remains permanently on file with the clerk of the court where you can obtain a certified copy for a nominal fee.

17.9 Is there anything else I should be doing after my divorce?

The following postdivorce checklist is helpful in considering many actions that may need to be addressed in your particular circumstances.

Postdivorce Checklist Continued

Property

_____Confirm necessary quitclaim deeds and real estate transfer statements have been filed with the county.

_____Refinance real property within the time frame specified by the decree of dissolution.

_____Complete the exchange of personal property.

_____Transfer the title on vehicles.

_____Transfer or close bank accounts and safe-deposit boxes.

_____Transfer investment accounts, stocks, and bonds.

_____Review beneficiary designations on retirement and financial accounts for any needed changes.

Property Settlement

_____Comply with property settlement payments in a timely manner pursuant to your decree.

Insurance

_____Review life insurance beneficiary designation for any needed changes.

_____Obtain COBRA or other needed health insurance.

_____Notify your medical insurance provider of your divorce.

_____Make sure your vehicle is insured in your name.

Debts and Liabilities

_____Cancel joint accounts or charge cards, or remove the name of your former spouse.

Parenting Plan

_____Notify your child's school of the noncustodial parent's address.

_____If you are the noncustodial parent, notify child's school of your desire to be notified of events, receive duplicate copies of report cards, etc.

Postdivorce Checklist   Continued

Child Support and Alimony

_____If ordered to pay support, provide original Notice to Withhold Income form to your employer and file a copy with the clerk.

_____A new Notice will be required each time you change employers.

_____Make sure payments are made in a timely manner.

_____Make sure that payments are documented. No cash.

Child-Care and Uninsured Medical Expenses

_____Set up a tracking-and-filing system to keep full and complete records regarding these financial matters.

Tax Matters

_____Notify your employer of the change in your exemption status (complete a new W-4).

_____If necessary, complete IRS Form 8822 for change of address and also notify the Tennessee Department of Revenue.

_____Refer to IRS Publication 504, "Divorced or Separated Individuals" for other questions.

Attorney Fees

_____Contact the law firm's account manager to make payment arrangements for any fees owed to the firm.

_____If your former spouse was ordered to pay a portion of your attorney fees, note that you remain responsible for the payment of your attorney fees, including any applicable interest, until the account is paid.

_____If you have been ordered to pay your former spouse's attorney, make payments through your attorney.

Postdivorce Checklist   Continued

Name Change

If you changed your name:

_____Contact the Social Security Administration (SSA) to complete an Application for Social Security Card (Form SS-5). The SSA will notify the IRS of your name change when your new Social Security card is issued.

_____Notify people and places regarding your name change. (*see* question 17.9).

Estate Planning

_____Schedule an appointment with your attorney to update or prepare your will, powers of attorney, and other important estate-planning documents.

In Closing

Now, pause and take a deep breath. Acknowledge yourself for the courage you have shown in examining your unique situation, needs, and goals. Now, you are facing your future—recasting yourself into a new life. You are looking more closely at your living situation, the needs of your children, your financial security, and your personal growth and healing. You are clearly seeing your situation, and being realistic about what you now need. You are taking action to explore new possibilities.

It is time to take inventory of the lessons learned, goals met, and action yet to take. Celebrate each of those steps forward and be gentle with yourself over the occasional misstep backward. You have transitioned through this time when everything is reduced to the core of you. Gone are the familiar habits of your marriage. With every day moving closer to the completion of your divorce, your grief will begin to subside and your energy improve as you move toward a fresh start. All the best to you as you accomplish this life journey!

Glossary

Affidavit: A written statement of facts made under oath and signed before a notary public. Affidavits are used primarily when there will not be a hearing in open court with live testimony. The attorney will prepare an affidavit to present relevant facts. Affidavits may be signed by the parties or in some cases by witnesses. The person signing the affidavit may be referred to as the *affiant.*

Alimony: Court-ordered spousal support payments from one party to another, often to enable the recipient spouse to become economically independent.

Allegation: A statement that one party claims is true

Answer: A written response to the petition for divorce. It serves to admit or deny the allegations in the complaint and may also make claims against the opposing party. This is sometimes called a *responsive pleading.* An answer should be filed within thirty days of either (a) the complaint being served by the sheriff or (b) the defendant's voluntary appearance being filed with the court.

Appeal: The process by which a higher court reviews the decision of a lower court. In Tennessee family law cases, a person will first file an appeal with the Tennessee Court of Appeals. After that appeal is decided there may be a further appeal to the Tennessee Supreme Court.

Application to modify: A party's written request to the court to change a prior order regarding custody, child support, alimony, or any other order that the court may change by law

Child support: Financial support for a child paid by the noncustodial parent to the custodial parent

Complaint: The first document filed with the clerk of the court in an action for divorce, separation, or paternity. The complaint sets forth the facts on which the requested relief is based.

Contempt of court: The willful and intentional failure of a party to comply with a court order, judgment, or decree. Contempt may be punishable by a fine or jail.

Contested case: Any case in which the parties cannot reach an agreement. A contested case will result in a trial to have the judge decide disputed issues.

Court order: A court-issued document setting forth the judge's orders. An order can be issued based upon the parties' agreement or the judge's decision. An order may require the parties to perform certain acts or set forth their rights and responsibilities. An order is put in writing, signed by the judge, and filed with the court.

Cross-examination: The questioning of a witness by the opposing counsel during trial or at a deposition, in response to questions asked by the other lawyer

Custody: The legal right and responsibility awarded by a court for the possession, care, and decision making for minor children.

Decree of dissolution: A final court order dissolving the marriage, dividing property and debts, ordering support, and entering other orders regarding finances and the minor children

Defendant: The responding party to a divorce; the party who did not file the complaint initiating the divorce

Deposition: A witness's testimony taken out of court, under oath, and in the presence of lawyers and a court reporter. If a person gives a different testimony at the time of trial, he or she can be impeached with the deposition testimony; that is, statements made at a deposition can be used to show untruthfulness if a different answer is given at trial.

Direct examination: The initial questioning of a witness in court by the lawyer who called him or her to the stand

Discovery: A process used by attorneys to discover information from the opposing party for the purpose of fully assessing a case for settlement or trial. Types of discovery include interrogatories, requests for production of documents, and requests for admissions.

Dissolution: The act of terminating or dissolving a marriage

Glossary

Equitable distribution of property: The method by which real and personal property and debts are divided in a divorce. Given all economic circumstances of the parties, Tennessee law requires that marital property and debts be divided in a fair and reasonable manner.

Ex parte: Usually in reference to a motion, the term used to describe an appearance of only one party before the judge, without the other party being present. For example, an *ex parte* restraining order may be granted immediately after the filing of a complaint for divorce.

Hearing: Any proceeding before the court for the purpose of resolving disputed issues between the parties through presentation of testimony, affidavits, exhibits, or argument

Hold-harmless clause: A term in a court order that requires one party to assume responsibility for a debt and to protect the other spouse from any loss or expense in connection with it, as in to hold harmless from liability

Interrogatories: Written questions sent from one party to the other that are used to obtain facts or opinions related to the divorce

Joint custody: The shared right and responsibility of both parents awarded by the court for possession, care, and decision making for minor children

Mediation: A process by which a neutral third party facilitates negotiations between the parties on a wide range of issues

Motion: A written application to the court for relief, such as temporary child support, custody, or restraining orders

Notice of hearing: A written statement sent to the opposing lawyer or spouse listing the date and place of a hearing and the nature of the matters that will be heard by the court. In Tennessee, one party is required to give the other party reasonable notice of any court hearing.

Party: The person in a legal action whose rights or interests will be affected by the divorce. For example, in a divorce the parties include the wife and husband.

Pending: During the case. For example, the judge may award you temporary support while your case is pending.

Petitioner: A term formerly used to refer to the plaintiff or person who files the complaint seeking a divorce

Plaintiff: The person who files the complaint initiating a divorce

Pleadings: Documents filed with the court seeking a court order

Qualified domestic relations order (QDRO): A type of court order that provides for direct payment from a retirement account to a former spouse

Request for production of documents: A written request for documents sent from one party to the other during the discovery process

Sequester: To order prospective witnesses out of the courtroom until they have concluded giving their testimony

Set off: A debt or financial obligation of one spouse that is deducted from the debt or financial obligation of the other spouse

Settlement: The agreed resolution of disputed issues

Show cause: Written application to the court to hold another person in contempt of court for violating or failing to comply with a current court order

Stipulation: An agreement reached between parties or an agreement by their attorneys

Subpoena: A document delivered to a person or witness that requires him or her to appear in court, appear for a deposition, or produce documents. Failure to comply could result in punishment by the court. A subpoena requesting documents is called a subpoena *duces tecum.*

Temporary restraining order (TRO): An order of the court prohibiting a party from certain behavior. For example, a temporary restraining order may order a person not to transfer any funds during a pending divorce action.

Trial: A formal court hearing in which the judge will decide disputed issues raised by the parties' pleadings.

Under advisement: A term used to describe the status of a case, usually after a court hearing on a motion or a trial, when the judge has not yet made a decision

Index

Index

IRS Publication 529, Miscellaneous Deductions, 176

J

joint income tax return, 173
judge, 100–104
  court, role in, 189
  deposition read by, 63
  infidelity, view on, 5
  picking, 19
  property settlement agreement, approval of, 155
  spouse's attendance in chambers of, 180
jurisdiction, 35
jurisdictional requirements, 5–6

K

kidnapping, *see* abduction

L

language of law used by attorney, 34–35
laws, 34–35, 68
lawyer, *see* attorney
legal assistant, 39–40
legal fees, free, 46–47, *see also* fees
legal name, restoration of, 20, 196–197
legal team, 41–42, *see also* attorney; support professionals
life insurance, 160–161
liquid assets, 147
litigation, *see* court; divorce process
live-in-partner, 108, 127, *see also* significant other
loans, student, 165
location for divorce, 6, *see also* residential requirements
loving feelings towards spouse, 25

M

maiden name, restoration of, 20, 196–197
mail, negotiations through, 75–76
marital dissolution agreement, 154–155
marriage
  compensation for wrong doings during, 43
  decree of dissolution of, 20, 35
  dissolution of, 7–12, 34 (*see also* divorce process)
  saving, 21–22
married filing a joint return filing status, 172
married filing a separate return filing status, 172
mediation and negotiation, 67–77, *see also* negotiations; settlement conference
  abuse and, 72–73
  attorney's role in, 74–75
  child/children attending, 74
  collaborative divorce *vs.*, 68
  communication during, 71
  defined, 68
  delays in divorce resulting from, 69–70
  differentiating between, 68
  failure of, 75
  fees for, 49–50, 70
  goals of, 70
  length of time for, 69
  mandatory, 72
  mediator for, 73
  payment for, 75
  preparing for, 74
  process of, 69
  for settlement agreement, 70–72
  spouse's attendance to, 27–28

214

in court, 186–187
during initial consultation, 37
when seeing attorney, 22, 56
petitioner, 35
petition for divorce, 7, 15, *see
also* divorce complaint
photographs to help judge
determine child custody, 111
plaintiff, 12–13
police involvement for
noncompliance with
parenting time, 117
postdivorce checklist, 197–200
postnuptual agreement, 34
premarital agreement, 153, *see
also* prenuptial agreement
premarital assets, 147–148
premarital debt, 166
premarital property, 147–148
prenuptial agreement, 34, 153
prescription medication, 24,
106
pretrial conference, 184
pretrial order, 184
pride, 27
primary caregiver, proving,
104–105
primary residential parents, 89
private detective for proving
affair, 107
private elementary school,
130
property, 146–149, *see also*
property, division of
community, 140
personal, 145
transfer of, 170
values of, determining, 149–
150
property, division of, 139–
155, *see also* assets; house/
home; property; settlement
agreement
bank accounts, 146–148, 150

of business, 151–152
collections, 145–146
community property and,
140
contesting, 149
death and, 155
debts and, 154
engagement ring, 148
of future earnings, 150–151
marital dissolution agreement
for, 154–155
out-of-state, 147
prenuptial agreement and,
153
process of, 140
property settlement agreement for, 155
stocks, 147, 150, 152–153
property settlement agreement,
153, 155
alimony and, differentiating
between, 135–136
judgments for, 196
payment for, 196
taxes and, 170
pro rata, 129
pro se, 2
protection order, 80–83
psychologists, 38–39, 50

Q
Qualified Domestic Relations
Order (QDRO), 157
questions asked during
deposition, 63–64
quitclaim deed, 144

R
refinancing mortgage, 167
reimbursement for child care,
44–45
relocation, out-of-state, 85,
117–118, 127, 137
remarriage, 127, 136
remorse, 23
rental income, 124

Index

About the Author

Eric J. Burch is an attorney in private practice with the firm Burch and Stanley, P.C. in Manchester, Tennessee. He has practiced law in Tennessee for more than fifteen years. He graduated from the University of Tennessee, earning his bachelor's degree in 1995 and doctorate of jurisprudence in 1998.

Burch formed his law firm in 2003. The focus of his practice is exclusively litigation with an emphasis on divorce and personal injury litigation.

Burch and his wife, Melissa, have three children, Auggie, Abigail, and Sam. In his spare time, Burch enjoys golfing and coaching his children's athletic teams.

He may be reached through his website:
www.ericjburch.com.

Divorce Titles from Addicus Books

Visit our online catalog at www.AddicusBooks.com

Divorce in Alabama: The Legal Process, Your Rights, and What to Expect $21.95

Divorce in Arizona: The Legal Process, Your Rights, and What to Expect. $21.95

Divorce in California: The Legal Process, Your Rights, and What to Expect $21.95

Divorce in Connecticut: The Legal Process, Your Rights, and What to Expect $21.95

Divorce in Georgia: The Legal Process, Your Rights, and What to Expect $21.95

Divorce in Illinois: The Legal Process, Your Rights, and What to Expect $21.95

Divorce in Louisiana: The Legal Process, Your Rights, and What to Expect $21.95

Divorce in Mississippi: The Legal Process, Your Rights, and What to Expect. $21.95

Divorce in Nebraska: The Legal Process, Your Rights, and What to Expect—2nd Edition $21.95

Divorce in Nevada: The Legal Process, Your Rights, and What to Expect. $21.95

Divorce in New Jersey: The Legal Process, Your Rights, and What to Expect $21.95

Divorce in New York: The Legal Process, Your Rights, and What to Expect $21.95

Divorce in Tennessee: The Legal Process, Your Rights, and What to Expect $21.95

Divorce in Texas: The Legal Process, Your Rights, and What to Expect. $21.95

Divorce in Virginia: The Legal Process, Your Rights, and What to Expect $21.95

Divorce in Washington: The Legal Process, Your Rights, and What to Expect $21.95

Divorce in West Virginia: The Legal Process, Your Rights, and What to Expect $21.95

To Order Books:
Visit us online at: www.AddicusBooks.com
Call toll free: (800) 352-2873

Addicus Books
P. O. Box 45327
Omaha, NE 68145

Addicus Books is dedicated to publishing books
that comfort and educate.

.